the way of the grace-filled heart

TRAVEL THE UNBROKEN PATH OF LIGHT AND LOVE

catherine grace landry

Satiama
PUBLISHING

satiamapublishing.com

The Way of the Grace-filled Heart
by Catherine Grace Landry

Copyright 2020, Catherine Grace Landry
and Satiama Publishing

Published and distributed by Satiama Publishing,
a service mark of Satiama, LLC
(www.satiamapublishing.com)
PO Box 1397
Palmer Lake, CO 80133

ISBN: 978-1-7349898-5-4 (print)
978-1-7349898-6-1 (e-book)

1. New Thought 2. Inspiration and Personal Growth
3. Personal Development

Written by Catherine Grace Landry
Graphic Design by Vision Design Studio
Cover Design by Anouk Landry
Copyright 2020, Catherine Grace Landry
and Satiama Publishing

For more information about Catherine Grace Landry, visit catherinegracelandry.com.

For more information about Satiama Publishing, visit satiamapublishing.com.

PRINTED IN CHINA
1 2 3 4 5 6 7 8 9 10

For R

… for those who came before…
… for those who cannot speak…

Contents

Foreword

One of humanity's oldest and most profound journeys is the seeker's quest to the inner self. This is a journey that we often embark on to satisfy our need to understand what it is that is greater than ourselves, what gives our life meaning or significance beyond the mundane, what is our role in the cosmic-Divine, and who we really are in the core of our essence. From the earliest time mankind has sought the answers to these questions, finding many ways to explain both the physical and occult world in which we each find ourselves, and employing many different ways to assign and define our human experience. Through cave paintings, ancient and modern rituals, the oral history of cultures and tribes, creed and superstition, to formal thought systems we call religions, we are each continuing in our search, even including those who don't believe in the existence of anything else other than just *us*.

The Way Series is about the destination of this journey. Beginning with *The Way of the Simple*

Soul, I told the story of an incredible message gifted to me by the Soul of an elderly man as he passed from this earth. It was the meaning of the Soul, its purpose, its intent, its role in our human lives as a vast repository of knowledge, perspective and choice. Along the way I offered brief stories of my own journey to deeply connect to and experience a very personal and intimate relationship with my Soul and how I was profoundly freed to live in authentic strength and joy.

My second book in the series, *The Way of the Lightkeeper*, offered the reader a stepping-stone into the portal of our heart's own connection to our Source, deepening our experience of the Light that sustains us. By opening and expanding my heart to truly understand that this connection is all-essential, I came to experience this third-dimensional world in a very different way, liberating me to see through the illusionary veil to understand how we are and always have been tethered, without disconnection, to this transcendent power.

The Way of the Grace-filled Heart, is the third and final part of the otherworldly message. It returns us to our earthly experience following the path of Light flowing from Source to us and to all living things, and back through us to Source in an infinite loop. A grace-filled heart offers us a thrilling ride on the magic carpet of our infinite possibility. This is not a finite destination, but an expanding experience of the truth of who we are. Here we meet our Soul, uncover our unlimited memory, finally begin to understand our magnificent and staggering potential and live within the stream of grace that is truly the fabric of our earthly experiences. It flows in all directions at all times with no limits, borders or boundaries.

A grace-filled heart invites us to live in empathic oneness with Source, which is our true essence. The Light opens us to who we really are – co-creators without limitation, love without expectation, judgment or definition, free and sovereign spiritual beings, Light that cannot be diminished.

If you, the reader, have walked the path from my first book to this present one, I thank you for sharing the 'road' with me, for allowing me to bring forward these chronicles to those for whom I might hold a torch to light your own path, and for acting upon your spiritual thirst to find your own answers.

May you find freedom and peace in the Oneness of Light that is truly your birthright.

Catherine Grace Landry
July 2020

In another time...

A woman crests the hill. She stands tall, silent, watchful, unmoving. In a small valley below rests the place of her childhood. The place that holds her memory.

The breeze is more benevolent than she remembers. But she had been a young child when last she stood in this place. Yet even now the breeze brings memories. It conjures tastes, smells, images.

There is the lake, the house, the porch. The wind murmurs gently through the centre of the house, spiraling through the missing front door and out through the back. Some days the house basked in the warmth. Others it shivered in the icy cold blowing off the surrounding islands and lagoons. Just as she used to do.

A labyrinth of adventures is contained in those tiny bits of land, captured in that crystal ball of time, swirling around the house that was the centre of that universe.

She walks down the hill. Her steps are sure, the path is clear and worn smooth. She circles the house. Long-ago players draw breath and swirl around her like dancers in the mist. Her memories pulse in time with her steps.

Out of the corner of her vision, a child races into view, laughing and clapping her hands as she chases an imaginary spirit. As she flew by, the house lifted its groaning timbers and stood tall and proud and protective once again. The girl looked back, smiled a secret smile, then skipped away and disappeared into the mist.

The woman walks down to the shore. She stares into the waters that are at once shallow and yet also deep. More memories crowded. Like a slow-motion movie of the hours spent perched on a log, on a mission, searching the watery depths for treasure. There was nothing of strangeness here, for at one time it teamed with life, her life.

The house is abandoned now. The lagoon is no longer peaceful. All is sunk in on itself, boards bent, land decaying, no little creatures running here and there. The bubble she lived within has moved on, leaving a lonely structure to the mercy of the wind and the waves.

Is all this because she is no longer there? Nothing is dead, only dormant, the life force resting and slumberous, waiting for…

… the story… the seeker… a thousand sacred fires … the songs of our Souls singing on the wind…

In the pulsing echoes of our stories glows the power that pulls us into our hearts. We are all storytellers. Our life is the sum of the stories we imagine, the stories we tell, and the stories we believe. The stories we tell are the legacy of our memories. The stories we imagine create our future.

We live life as a procession of stories. In each moment is a tiny and unfolding tale. One that we store , or release to the wind. The qualities of that story enter into the web of frequencies that are interlacing imperceptibly between us.

Our lives are about the experience and the sharing of our experiences. It is about the sharing of love in all its forms. Love is an extension of our essence, which is Light. We pulse our Light out into the world through the stories that we create, those that we give voice. We emit a spark each time we think a thought, say a word, laugh or smile. We fill the world with Light as a lighthouse splits the fog.

Through stories we find our way to our hearts. Our stories can help others find their way to their hearts. For beneath these stories, deep within the vast caverns of our inner planes, lies a crystal stream that bubbles with the truth of our Self, our primal essence. We can choose our stories to ignore our essence or we can choose our essence and live its stories.

Our primal essence is our very own Light. It lives within us in the womb. It peeps out from our eyes as babies. All of our life we play with it. We bury it, open it, close it, box it, ignore it, explore it, do a million things with it. For each of these things we do with our Light, we create a story.

We live life as a procession of stories. In each moment is a tiny and unfolding tale.

The stories we tell are often related to genetics, the stories we think are often related to traditions, and the stories we believe are often answers to questions we have held mutely within ourselves. We are the product of these, yet, at the end of all things, these are simply stories.

Beyond our quest for meaning, purpose, or faith there is a space without time or dimension that is a pulsing pinpoint of knowing. It prompts our hands to be outstretched, our words to be spoken, our thoughts to be heard, our emotions to be expressed. It is the deep inner river of infinite grace.

Grace is invisible, yet we feel it flow through the stories we live. In the sensations of these, we can taste, smell, touch, embrace.

Moments of grace fill our life with love, with Light, with wisdom. For what is grace, but the Light of our Source sent to guide our hearts in the way of its own perfect love.

Grace is the dispensation and suspension of man-made laws. It calls upon the powers of our Source to help us release restrictions and allow its primal flow. In the flow of grace, there are tendrils of truths, insights, answers, gifts, that reach out with invisible power, magnetizing our hearts, electrifying our minds.

The pathway of infinite grace flows far beyond understanding. With our intellect, we learn, ultimately to get forget what was learned. Recall that at some point in our past we learned to walk and talk. We learned our place in our family, our culture. We learned the expectations of our roles in our workplace and our family. We learned basic laws like gravity and how we are to manage our physical self within this 3-dimensional earth structure. With these lessons we came to understand how to be a human, and not a chicken or a fox.

We learned these functions so well that after a time, we no longer needed to remember in our minds how to do them. We automatically, instinctively and unconsciously perform the tasks of being a human within the units of our family, society and global community. We become so entwined with our learnings that we become them.

Such is the way with grace. The grace-filled heart teaches the mind to trust in the heart's integration and absorption of its learnings of love and Light.

Grace is Light in action. It is purely a sensory knowing. The heart is its pulsing core. Here we experience the living sensation of grace. In turn, our hearts pour grace outwards in a flow that ripples farther than we can ever conceive. We are not simply from a unified Source. We are that Source.

We are a reflective mirror of that Source's essence, reflecting the Light which creates us, seemingly, as individuals. We are its Love. We are its Light. The flow of grace is our Source, filling us with its knowledge and asking us to open our hearts to its freedom and peace.

Entering the vast, inner planes of our heart, we find ourselves in an infinite universe. Here lies the path of the multi-dimensional journey to oneness with our Source, known by many names: the way of peace, the way of Light, the way of the holy ones, the way of love, the way of our Source and so on. These are not the physical spaces we experience here on earth. They are like bands of frequencies. We can tune ourselves, as we tune a radio, to different bandwidths to receive different frequencies.

In these bands we meet our Soul, experience unlimited memory, and glimpse our vast potential. In these frequencies we meet the grace that flows upon our earthly experiences. It flows like a river of silky water burbling over mossy planes, and smooth stones, in a vast delta, yet in all directions at all times. It has no chapters, divisions, sequences. It has no limits, borders or boundaries.

Grace wishes us to step over the divisions, ignore the periods, collapse the chapters of the stories we build up within our minds and beliefs. It calls us to look through eyes that see only an endless and unlimited field with no fences, structures, or hedges. Grace offers us infinite possibility.

*Grace is the dispensation and
suspension of man-made laws.*

Where are the divisions to empathy? This family versus a stranger's family? Where are the walls to compassion? This person and not that one? Where are the gates to love that we open only under certain conditions. Where are the barriers strong enough to block the flow of grace?

As with grace…so with this book… without sequence or linear direction… begin and end wherever you wish…

I dreamed of Africa...

The light was golden, the grasses were golden, pockets of golden sand shifted here and there. The space before me was vast, wild, with a stillness that defied description.

There were unusually shaped trees circling ponds of life-giving water. The sky was a colour I had not seen anywhere else on Earth. There were animals, large and small, ambling along, nibbling the grasses, sleeping in the shady hollows.

I was perplexed as to why I was there, for it was a landscape that had no need of humans. I shuffled along with a sense that I was not alone. There were other beings, spirits, peacefully going about their

11

business, whatever that might be. I was of no concern to them at all. Just another being walking the plains.

I came upon a group of large animals, looking something like wildebeests perhaps. It was dusk by this time, the cool air was settling in, the herd was quietly circling around its young as if to say goodnight, time for sleep.

There was a rustling to one side, and I noticed a lioness, very calmly and quietly observing the scene. She seemed to be waiting for something.

The herd was not at all alarmed by her presence. It was as if they knew she was there, they knew what she needed, but they all seemed to sense that she would get what she needed without much disturbance to the group.

As if on an otherworldly cue, a bull ambled her way. It was old, tired, haggard. It wandered into a stand of trees and collapsed on its side. The lioness quietly followed. She looked at him and he looked at her.

In this beautiful dance of life and death, the hungry lioness waited patiently for the old bull to lay down and sigh his last breath out into the living world.

He knew she waited and didn't prolong his or her suffering. With intuitive knowing that it was his time to leave and her time to prosper, he willingly laid down his life.

Feel the Creator's pulse

*… listen… there is a pulse… mesmerizing
and infinite… expanding and contracting…
a breath, a whisper, a growling, a thundering…
an eternal sigh wafting through time…*

The pulse of the cosmos is a never-ending cycle of construction, deconstruction, and reconstruction. It is life. It is death. In this pulse are the magnetic and electric, the projective and the receptive forces, what we call masculine and feminine, yet so much greater than these.

In this cosmic flow all happens at different intervals yet also all at once. A seething miasma of movement that appears chaotic. We cannot hear it, taste it, touch it, or see it. Yet, we sense it deeply within as a flutter calling to us, so softly, "Come ride the wave. We are one, you and I. Flow with me in the ecstasy of being."

We subconsciously chase that flow through time and space. We feel it in our breathing. In our inner vision, in our inner ears. It pulses in multi-dimensional geometric symbols, from the tiny to the massive. How often we are mesmerized by a fire's twisting flames or snowflakes twirling on the breeze, because they move, pulse, flow with unexpected yet beautiful twists and turns. They are reminders that we also move in the very same way.

The pulse of our blood is the river of the cosmos within us. This is the place within where we may feel the fullness of ourselves beating in time to our Source.

Close your eyes, rest in your heartbeat, and you can feel the movement. Our heart mirrors the pulsing of all things and invites us to live naturally according to this rhythm, if we choose. In this vessel, the heart, we return to the primal matrix of our existence. All dimensions at once, all directions at once, no time, no space.

The pulse of our blood is the river of the cosmos within us. This is the place within where we may feel the fullness of ourselves beating in time to our Source. It gives us the sensation of being in all dimensions of time and space simultaneously.

In our heart we feel this pulse most strongly. It is in this space that we tune to our Creator and to all of creation. It is here that we feel we are one of those creations, and we are one with all.

This is the pulse that lifts us above the primitive. Like the dance of the snowflake, we can dance this cosmic rhythm in our lives here on this planet. If we halt this rhythm, we create a block to our Self. Our psyche, mind, body, all parts and elements of our being, naturally move with energy currents along continuous patterns.

Purposely blocking this movement, stopping our imagination from playing, restricting our minds from exploring beyond our current knowledge, creates a rigidity and inertia. Over time, this becomes as a solid mountain that takes herculean efforts to set in motion once again.

Our heart is not a generator of emotion, as we have come to believe. It is so far beyond this. The heart holds a new type of map for us to learn to read. It holds a map to guide us to the infinite, to our Source. It shows us how to find our Source and how to bring back the Light of Source to our Self and to all the world around us. We are eternally connected to Source as is everything around us also connected.

Entering the heart and communing with our Soul unveils this magical map that stares us plainly in the face, waiting for us to insert the key in the lock, open the door and travel its pathways. Its answers will present themselves if we will hold still and abandon for a moment our sense of a linear existence.

It is an illusion to think we are fully linear. This illusion is based on our ability to focus our thinking clearly on one aspect of something at a time and create for it a forward marching momentum. In fact, we are a continuous outpouring of non-linear activity, moving as a laminar-like energy flow.

Laminar flow translated into human thought patterns might be similar to states of reflection or contemplation where all simply pulses within us in a seemingly random way, outputting continuous waves of raw data. We pull information, knowledge, understanding from this raw data, so to speak. From time to time we mold this raw data to create a structure, an objective, a physical action, or speech. Beneath that focussed data we have pulled up to create a linear action, all else is continuing to move in a seemingly chaotic flow of energy.

All the energy of life is moving at different frequencies and rates of vibration. Within one, two, and three-dimensional reality we are able to physically move in only one direction at a time. We can move forwards or backwards, side to side, up or down, and in and out. In other dimensions we can physically move in ways we cannot fully comprehend here. We may not be able to physically leave our bodies to experiment with this, but we can imagine. To experience a taste of this, we place our mind in the service of our heart.

Our Soul is multidimensional. Our heart is the bridge to these other dimensions. It is our own little quantum generator. It can bend and pulse like a tesseract. It is what gives us the image in our minds of the infinite, the faint whispers of vague memories. An undulating. A compressing and stretching like an elastic band. Moving and morphing and never still. The pulse of the universe.

I dreamed of a vortex...

I was surrounded by red rocks. It was dry and desert-like yet teeming with life. There were people, towns, activity at all levels. Adults bustling about their businesses, children off to school, tourists driving around chattering and taking photos.

There was so much activity it made me dizzy. My head was swimming, my body was unsettled. Something was very wrong.

I took myself for a walk into the quiet of the hills and sat meditatively under a shady tree pondering the beautiful display of nature spread out below me. Green trees, jagged red rocks, rolling valleys.

There were so many humans, it looked like a frenetic hive of ants far below my perch.

One would consider it to be a normal scene yet there were swirling vortexes of energy all around this activity. It was at once lovely and disturbing. In the silence, so far above, I could see this more clearly.

Suddenly, a medicine man appeared in front of me. He was similar or perhaps the same as a medicine man-type being who has appeared to me before in dreams.

An image of a tangled ball of yarn appeared before me.

He said: "Do not mold your frequency to that of others. Hold your own. Be in peace in your heart."

Rest in the eye of the storm

…eye of the storm… a quiet… a stillness…
a void… where all activity comes to rest…

There is a swirling fog of shadows around our heart, light and dark, strength and weakness. It rages as a hurricane circling the eye of the storm. Our heart is the storm's center that transforms these external winds to stillness.

In the refuge of this Light-filled vessel nothing can knock us down. We feel the grief, pain, devastation, joy, wonder, excitement of our life as it flows within and around us. At times, these build to peaks of intensity we feel we cannot survive.

In our hearts there is a central calm foundation for us to rest, where we transform this intensity and allow it to naturally ebb.

In this calm state we can make sense of the depths of the valleys and the heights of the peaks of our life situations. While these peaks and valleys are the natural ebb and flow of the circumstances and situations in our lives, they are not us. While they may be events our Soul came to experience, the calm eye of our heart maintains our balance through all storms.

Source is the central point of the infinite cosmos from which all emanates. Its primal declamations bring forth the flow of all possibility and potentiality. Our heart is fashioned to be this primal point within our human structure. It is the centre of intelligence that allows us to both sense and think, simultaneously. Pre-form, this state of all possibility and potentiality lives in the eye of our hearts, much like a wish, or imaginative whimsy. Once a solid form is realized, through structured thought and action, there are no more possibilities and potentialities for that form. But it can be modified or changed by returning to the place of original potentiality and creating anew.

The energies emanating directly from Source are free form, shifting and changing, constantly in motion prior to becoming a manifested structure, thought, or action. This type of flow appears to us as undisciplined, undirected chaos. Chaos is a very uncomfortable state to the human mind that functions on the basis of creating order, linear process, and solid structure.

In chaos we feel lost. Yet we dwell in this unstructured place from the beginning of our lives, from swimming in the amniotic fluid of the womb, to the young years of percieving our world as a flow of events yet to be understood. This formless essence is where we are meant to spend much of our energies as it is the place from which we can observe, discern, imagine, and grow. From this place we make our choices to either link to our mind and create in form, or rest here indefinitely in potential.

This free-form flow is our heart's natural element. We find our essence by relaxing into or abandoning ourselves to this sensitive space, which is an extension of our Source. To experience this sensitive space, we must learn to awaken our sensory fields. The sensory fields are the infinite numbers of sensations, and grouped sensations, that happen through our skin, organs, bones, every particle of our mind/body/spirit being.

The core of our cells are firing continually, talking to our nerves, our blood, muscles, tissues, organs. Our cells react to our thoughts, our actions, our Soul, to the other dimensions we cannot see around us, and they fire off responses. The resulting sensations go far beyond our simple sense of touch, hearing, sight, smell and taste.

We can learn to lock on to the sensations brought about by something we are seeking. Imagine that the sensation of peace feels to you like a certain note on the piano. When you hear the sound of that note you are flooded with peaceful sensations. When we feel ourselves getting edgy, abrupt, angry, sarcastic, we can lock onto that re-membered frequency of peace and allow it to pull us into our heart. Responses such as anger, edgi-ness, irritability are the result of pulses within our sensory fields that are disharmonious.

The more we tune into and understand our sen-sory fields responses, we can accurately translate the situations we find ourselves in, and not fuel further negative responses. Irritation and abrupt behaviour is my go-to response when my sensory fields are telling me I am in contact with some-thing that is of a frequency field far out of tune with mine. Understanding the root of this be-havior allows me to take it into the calm eye of my heart. Relaxing here brings a softening of the abrupt edges, a melting, and a reset to ponder all possibilities and potentialities that we have just come in contact with, allowing a transformation.

Transformation takes place in the deep and secret chambers of the heart, the calm eye of the storm, the sensitive space. Transformation happens when elements of ourselves and our responses are magnetized into our heart. We must ask for it. We must want it. It is a voluntary action of opening and allowing.

Transformation involves the solar plexus (seat of our personal will), the mind (seat of our thought ability) and the heart.

Transformation does not happen in the blink of an eye. These blink of an eye moments have actually been prepared by small degrees over time through alignment of the will, the mind, and the heart. Our will must desire transformation. Our mind must be willing to apply a little abstract reason. Our heart must be open and allowing. These three vessels then align in the alchemical process that activates the transformation in the heart which then releases the new result.

Transformation sets us on a path beyond the cycles of fate, nature, pre-destiny, or whatever you choose to call it. Within this calm eye of the storm, we can sense the vastness of the pulsing cosmos and our part within it. Here we are unbound from the 'cross' of our own limiting beliefs. Hatred, judgement, and other restrictive alliances simply take up too much space. They leave us too little space for our own self-discoveries.

Dwelling in this calm eye of the still-point can purify, lighten, and uncomplicate our responses to our world. The exchange between us takes place in the still-point. It is a non-verbal exchange of giving and receiving. Before our mind tells us to give, receive, or take, there is a silent, free, and infinite flow of information.

Finding the calm eye of the storm within our heart allows us to respond by sharing as grace the flow of Light that gives us life.

We are accountable for how we respond to the affairs around us. We do not need to invite the complexity of our internal/external worlds into the silent chambers of our hearts. We cannot, and would not, want to uncomplicate our world, but we can uncomplicate our response, and our interface between our inner Self and our external world.

Finding the calm eye of the storm within our heart allows us to respond by sharing as grace the flow of Light that gives us life.

*I dreamed of a place far away
and long ago...*

*The wind was keening the voices of lost centuries. I
saw a man holding fast to the hand of a little girl.
They walked the shores of a wild and ancient sea.
The wind was whipping around them. The waves
were crashing on the beach by their feet.*

*The child played innocently, interested in all things
around her. She skipped, she ran, she bent to ex-
amine the shells and the seaweeds. Her gifts from
the sea. She twirled and scampered over the rocks
to inspect the tender green grasses shooting up in
the cracks.*

This giant of a man was filled with wonder as he watched over her, his tiny treasure. Her freedom was his greatest joy. She rushed to him with her gifts and her love for him filled the air.

The wind picked up. He lifted her effortlessly and held her securely to his chest. They stood motionless like this for a long time, each held to the other.

He pointed to the sea and spoke to her of times and places she will know when she grows, of times and places he experienced when he was young, and always of the dreams he carries in his heart.

This giant and this tiny child are locked in time. With her life she will give to him the meaning of time. Her time. The time to soften, the time to strengthen, the time to nurture and imagine. In turn he will give to her his time. The time to protect, and to build, to structure and expand.

Together they will create what they cannot yet dream of.

They are two sides of the same being, innocence and wisdom, masculine and feminine, eternally inseparable. They have no need to label one or the other, no need to intellectually understand one or the other.

They hold one shared intent. The ebb and flow of creation...

You hold the space between

… the space between… invisible… intangible,
tangible… layers of vibrating space…
X marks the spot…

Something floats in and around the cells of our body, the chambers of our hearts, the air we breathe. It twines in and around the words on these pages. It is the space between all things.

Take a moment to visualize a phantom-like separation point between your internal world and the external world around you. Visualize a point where these two areas touch. Visualize another person standing in front of you and imagine this point in the space between you.

Call to mind the image of an infinity loop, the figure eight on its side. Now imagine that the outside curve of the loop begins in your heart and the opposite outside curve of the loop resides in the other person's heart. Imagine the point in the middle where the two looping lines cross. This is the point that exists precisely between you and the other. It is the 'X marks the spot' where you end and the other begins, and vice-versa. This intersection point is where your reality meets the next person's reality.

There is such an intersection point between all things. When two objects come into each other's orbit, there is always a point where they meet, a cosmic Venn diagram intersecting two individual spheres of energy. This intersection point is the third great force that propels our world.

Most of us tend to believe in very simple terms about the physical structure of our world, that it marches nicely along two by two in the polarity of the projective and the receptive, and the duality of oppositions, the inner/outer, up/down, for-ward/backward, side to side, right/wrong.

*Our Soul vibrates strongly within
and all around us even when we do
not believe or comprehend what it is.*

We are much more than a world of dual forces, we are a world of multiple forces. This intersection between all living things is much more than a simple point, it is an extremely powerful force.

There is a constant stream of frequencies moving outwards to another and then back into us in an infinite loop of sharing and seeking. It creates what we call the collective, the sum of all the intersection points. This collective builds like a set of harmonics and rebounds back to us, then redoubles the harmonics to create a larger and larger bandwidth of frequency as it bounces back out from us.

Our Soul vibrates strongly within and all around us even when we do not believe or comprehend what it is. Beyond the conscious relationships between humans, the Souls of each connect through a subconscious bandwidth of energy frequencies. A superhighway of activity.

Listen to the conversations around us. The hum of stories, the exchange of information, knowledge, wisdom, even the tiniest bits carry sharing and comparing. What is this but the attempt of one Soul to commune with another? Seeking community is one of our most foundational urges.

We each seek the Soul in the other. We seek the depth of the other's understanding to compare or complete our own understanding. This originates in the inner planes of our hearts and exercises itself in the outer space between one physical being and another through our body language, our words, our actions. In turn, the other crosses this point into us through their emotions, actions, and words.

We have thousands of thoughts being processed and shaped, constantly evolving emotions, a myriad of energetic impulses contained within what we perceive as a physical body and its organs - particularly the mind and heart. Outside our physical bodies we are surrounded by 'others' – humans, plants, animals, earth, the elements, weather patterns, vehicles, electronics, and so on, each with its own instincts, responses, activities, agendas.

We clump together. We gather in groups, talk on phones, connect through social media. We seek a point of interface between the internal world of our psyche and Soul and the deep, wild place within the others where their essence dwells. We seek in the external world the projected internal world of all other sentient beings.

This point of intersection in the space between is a balance point, a fulcrum. We attempt to balance that point somehow so that one side does not overpower the other, tipping the fulcrum, either crashing out of control into the other, or falling away into total oblivion. We tend to work within several well-practised, comfortable patterns to navigate this point.

Typically, we either blast through that intersection with the full throttle of our inner complexities or we allow the external complexities of the world to blast through that point into our inner Self. We often bounce back and forth between the two, wondering what hit us. Sometimes we give up, not for lack of caring, but for lack of understanding how to make a dent of positive progress.

Yet, there are some who are not buffeted back and forth. They take instinctive and different action at the intersection point. Their inner psyches are in as much turmoil as the next person's and their external worlds are equally as complex. Yet they navigate between these with a simplicity that makes their lives appear so much more harmonious than others, and generally, they seem more content.

Their pattern has a different weave. There is a stop sign at the intersection between themselves and others. These people make a choice at that intersection, a choice to stop the unchecked flow between their inner and outer life. They apply a filter on all the comings and goings. If we could place words on their 'stop sign' they might be something like these: empathy, sympathy, compassion, mercy.

It is not so much the words or actions that they share with others, as it is the frequency upon which these float. They choose to open their heart to allow grace to flow through the intersection point between themselves and every other living entity.

A grace-filled world rests on the foundation of our choices.

By doing this, any negativity they may have felt inside does not spill unchecked into the intersection. It is instead tempered to allow the recipient to understand their concerns without being scorched to bitter ashes in the process. The waves of fear that wreak havoc in our outer world do not blast unchecked through the intersection to create bitter inner thoughts, forestalling rational analysis and right action.

At this intersection point – this powerful third force in our world of duality - is a major element involving a decision. A simple, uncomplicated decision. The decision is this: do I allow grace to flow through me or do I not? It IS a decision. It is not a gift that some are born with and others not. It is not a privilege that some receive grace and others do not. It is a force that can be activated by everyone simply by making the decision to activate it.

In every encounter we make this choice in the blink of an eye. We choose what to project through our thoughts, emotions, words, body language, and more. What will we choose? Anger, kindness, smiles, laughter, sacredness, profanity, love?

A grace-filled world rests on the foundation of our choices. When the decision is to allow grace to flow, the way forward is one of balance, stability, realized potential, positive growth, progress in our external world, and peace within.

I dreamed I was travelling...

We were stopped with roadblocks or traffic jams or something of that sort – it was very unclear. Someone suggested we take a detour over to the left, which we did.

We entered a foggy, misty place. We parked and left the car to enter a building. When we came out, we had drinks in hand, the sun was shining, and we proceeded to relax on a deck overlooking a lovely landscape of forest and lakes. Very summer cottage-style! It all seemed very normal, a nice summer day with friends.

Then it changed again.

One of us produced a substance and lazily sprinkled it far and wide through the air. The air shimmered and shifted and then settled once again.

The dream opened to a different scene. I was relaxing, half-asleep on a lounge chair, enjoying the peace and quiet, when a tree walked up to me – yes, a tree. It looked at me and I regarded it.

We exchanged thoughts without speaking. I laid my hand on its bark in tenderness as I would a beloved child. It leaned in and brushed my head in affection. If it had been human, I am sure it would have winked broadly at me.

An animal that resembled a big cat, possibly a cougar or mountain lion, padded into my awareness. It curled up at my feet, its tail wrapped companionably around my legs, basking in the warm sunlight and the physical connection. I marvelled at the messages passing between us, creatures of such different species.

My tree leaned in again and sent me an answering thought. Of course, it had heard me! We were all communing without uttering a sound.

A being from the illumined dimensions beyond ours -- those I call Shining Ones -- peeked into the dream for a brief moment with a smile:

"This is how it was before fear entered the psyche of all creatures."

It was a tiny glimpse of the feeling of oneness with all creation, of the substance and vibration of the world before this time.

I woke up at that moment, smiling broadly and luxuriating in such serenity, joy, and Light throughout every cell of my body.

I am you...you are me

... what is in the Whole is in the one...
I am you... you are me... I am the Whole...
the Whole is me... convergence...

What is in one is in the Whole. This phrase in the personal "one" perspective means I am not alone, I am connected to all, six degrees of separation, no man is an island, and so on. This phrase examined from the 'Whole' perspective means there is a Whole, with links that connect all, a group consciousness, a web of living energy running through all living things.

The Whole is all of us and all of every living creature and we are but individuated facets of this

Whole. The idea that we are separate from this Whole is part of the sense we have that all on Earth functions in duality, two forces. This is an illusion based innocently upon the misconception that we are a human animal existing separately from the notion of a Soul, a spirit and a Source.

The Whole is by its definition the sum of the frequencies that are sent into it. The intersection points of all living things bounce both forward to the other and back to us and sideways, up and down and all around. The energy projected in the space between us is a bandwidth of frequencies, more like a field than a single point.

Our responsibility is to be in that Light, to open our hearts to flow as grace into the Whole.

The merging of these creates a massive convergence field carrying an altered and exponentially more powerful frequency than the tone or character of the individual frequencies. The whole is greater than the sum of its parts. The quality of this convergence field is what penetrates back into us.

What is in each one of us transfers into the field and converges with all others to create the web-like network we call collective consciousness. In other words, it not only penetrates the Whole, it becomes the Whole. You and I are the Whole, so whatever I am will ultimately be you as well. Not only what I *do* but what I *am* inside my psyche and Soul enters the Whole, becomes the field and then loops back to enter you.

In one, in the Whole. This is a result, but also a consequence. This Whole that has been created by all of us returns back to the individual - to either haunt us or liberate us. To change us for better or worse. We are all responsible for our own part in creating the Whole we exist within. We all have had a huge part to play in how the world got to where it is and how we move the world beyond this. We are each responsible for what we put into the Whole. We need to be sure that what is 'in' me is of a quality to sustain the strength and integrity of the Whole.

There is a vast significance to the responsibility and the consequence of this. The Whole is only as strong as the weakest energy being sent into it. Similar to a spider's web, each strand is connected with a specific type of fibre, woven to a specific strength to handle the activities that will happen on that web. If one strand is weaker, or breaks, the entire web will collapse under the weight of the spider's activities.

The quality of the whole structure of our families, businesses, societies, planet, and beyond is totally dependent on what our inner selves project into it, dependant on how we are doing on the inside of ourselves. Our heart values are the frequency that infuses the Whole and becomes the Whole, which then doubles back. It is a perpetual cycle, an unbreakable loop, like the multiplying effect of harmonics that build to an intensity that either shatters us all or brings transcendence.

Behind the smiles are we thinking, "I am afraid of this" or "I hate that person"? These are the real frequencies being projected to the world. What do we hold in our hearts?

In the expansion of our human-Soul partnership we delve into our psyches, offer up our blackest depths for cleansing and healing, explore our Light, and then reintegrate all our various bits and pieces in an ever-expansive spiral of experiences.

We learn shielding and cleansing techniques to keep frequencies that are not ours out of our personal energy fields. It is so important to not put up a shield at our own heart point despite the need to filter the flow back to us from the convergence field. The secure way to do this is to shift into the Light of our heart center, and project into the Whole a platform of Light. A force of wind moving strongly in one direction is difficult to counteract. A force-field of Light creates its own shield that negativity and fear cannot penetrate.

Our responsibility is to be in that Light, to open our hearts to flow as grace into the Whole. Our grace will hit the intersection point and converge with the group field. It carries its own alchemy. It does not need an external platform of good deeds created for the sake of feeling needed or useful, simply perfect unconditional love. To feed the Light into the Whole we simply need to hold it unwaveringly within our hearts, and allow it to flow to all around us.

I dreamed I was walking on the shore...

The light was the pale pink of early morning as the sun was just ascending over the horizon. The stillness crept silently into my being. I found myself perched rather precariously on the side of a pond. My eyes drifted shut as I contemplated the day ahead.

All of a sudden, I was transported through a portal and flying far out into the galaxy. When the dizzying motion ceased, I was floating amongst the stars looking down on the tiny blue dot that was Earth. A Shining One appeared in answer to a question I had not voiced.

She smiled with such love and beckoned me to look to the Earth at my physical self by the pond, trailing a hand in the water. Then she showed me the same image in the multi-dimensional view she could perceive.

She was standing with her hand on my head. Connected to her was a train-like string of Shining Ones. All of them connected through her to me, seated at the pond. They were sending healing frequencies into the web-like grid of frequencies around and within the earth.

The energy flowed right through me, through my hand and entered the water. She showed me how this energy then traveled at lightspeed through the earth from this one infusion in a water source. Water is the lifeblood of Earth.

She explained: "Earth is a unique place in the universe where free will is the governing law. We humans must give them permission to work through us and with us. We are their conduits. When we ask, the Light flows in abundance and healing is instant."

I am a channel. We are all channels for the flow of infinity...

Infinity beckons

*…infinity… loops, crosses… meanders, rushes…
splits and separates… mixes and mingles…*

Creation is an infinite loop unleashed to wander, explore, seek. It appears aimless, yet is full of purpose. It seeks any and all directions. It knows no parameters, boundaries, no single dimension. We are it and it is us. We seek it and it seeks us.

We all desire to be known. When we meet on a street we smile as if to say, "I know you, fellow Soul." We want to experience that reciprocation. We crave that momentary Soul-deep connection. This is the fuel that carries us forward, the thirst we seek to quench.

It is this interaction of shared fields that creates movement. Movement is the building block of creation. Two substances coming together and creating a friction that causes movement. Movement creates momentum, which translates within each of us to subtle shifts in thought and emotion, conveyed through the Whole.

The whole of our existence is an infinite, looping creation from Source to us, through us, out to all around us, returning back into us, filling us and flowing back to Source – to then repeat in one fluid, continuous and instantaneous flow.

Imagine this as a continuous pattern of infinity-loops flowing in all directions and dimensions of time and space, touching each and every one of the living beings in our cosmos. The loops never fade and they never close in any way that we can perceive, because we are fundamentally indivisible from our Source. They begin from Source and they conclude at Source in a perfect, unbroken motion.

Imagine the infinity loop that exists joins your heart to the next person's heart with the 'X marks the spot' in the space between. Now visualize where the loop runs in through the front of your heart. Imagine that it does not turn and go back out the front of your heart but continues on through the back of your heart and out to the person behind you. Visualize that there is now an X within your heart, as the crossing point of the loop. And now imagine that these looping lines go on into infinity in all directions, all at once, from the center of your heart, from the center of all hearts.

The point at which the loop finally rounds out and begins its journey back is the point where it touches our Source. The front end of the infinity loop continues as well, onwards through all created beings until it eventually is back at Source. This flow enters our heart and flows through us outwards to the next living being, and the next and the next. A continuous looping and crossing that begins and ends at Source. This is the net-

work of oneness, the grid of interconnected energy that contains the life force of all.

Our heart is our doorway, our portal to let this
loop in and pass it along. It is where we choose
to be actively connected, or not, to infinity. It can
be open and shut as we ask of it. It can be made
small, or large by our choice. Yet in the intelligent,
infinite scheme of creation this flow is meant to
be continuous, undammed, unstoppable, never
made small, never shut off. We are all one, whether we like it or not. We are created to share.

Light carries the spark of Source that gives us life.
We are Source's creation. It shares its delight in us
through the Light that streams through our Soul.
We feel its Light in our hearts as a kind of love.
A love vastly different from our human version,
which is built on reciprocity and power exchange.

Source's delight is a 'love for love's sake' kind of
love, that has no expectations or requirement for
return. It tells us that we are loved just as we are,

we are perfect and free to blossom as we choose, without the slightest hint of judgement.

We are in a time of remembering that our most powerful energy tool is not a crystal or an object, it is us. Our mind, thoughts, voices, gestures. We are connected to Source and all other sentient beings in our world through the infinity loop of our heart. This connection is a co-creative element between us.

As we are a unified being, I know what you need within your heart, and I provide it, as I am part of you. I do not know what job you need or where you need to live, or whether you should marry this one or that one. But I know your essence needs the same things as my essence, because we are of the same essence.

Our entire being is structured to attract and project this Light-Love we receive from Source. It is not meant to be soaked up and stopped within ourselves, as if we alone are the most important recipient. Like a river it was meant to flow outwards from us to everything around us.

Light in action we have named grace. The heart pours grace into the world and receives grace returned from the world. The heart pours the actions of grace back to Source and receives more grace from Source in return. The heart forwards this on in an eternal dance of Light. Be new, think new, make room for the new by opening the outward flow of the heart.

Our Soul seeks the other Soul. First, to share the knowledge of what it is; second, to assist it and every other being in the loop of infinity; third, to merge our Light. Ultimately to ride the loop through infinity back to our Source.

We do this, not by leaving the planet and returning to some distant place, but in our chosen human identity as one with all others. Not unified in a physical, mental or emotional sense.

Spiritually unified, which means knowing what we are, and that we each are fractals of the original emanation from Source.

We are in a time of remembering that our most powerful energy tool is not a crystal or an object, it is us.

I dreamed of a strange symbol...

It was like a strange form of sacred geometry. It was very bright and goldish-white. It hung suspended, unmoving in a void that undulated like the plasma on a computer screen as you run a finger over it.

I had never seen anything like this before. I stared intently at it, trying to match it to anything in my memory. It was so multi-dimensional I could not grasp the whole of it with my mind.

All of a sudden, the symbol began to rotate. It spun all around me and burrowed within me. I felt it link to the Light field in the diamond core of my physical self, and my cells seemed to blast apart.

My human self was dissolving. In one tiny corner of lucidity I may have felt a bit hysterical. I had this crazy image of the transporter machine from a Star Trek movie. Beam me up, Scotty!

At this point the symbol took off in an upwards direction, with me connected to it. It expanded my Light field and I expanded with it. We travelled deep into space, through the galaxies and universes, far, far beyond where I usually go in my dreams. I was a tiny dot, spinning ever more quickly through multiple dimensions.

Suddenly, we slowed and stopped. This was a place I had never traveled to before. Everything felt as if it were suspended rather than balanced on anything solid. There were fields of lights moving all around me.

One of these lights came very close and looked at me curiously, as if to say, "Mmm, what are you doing here?" It seemed perhaps I was in a place I was not supposed to be. It was so strange. I felt like a child caught with their hand in the candy jar, yet I sensed I had every right to be there.

In the next instant others joined in and conferred together. He had apparently determined I had shown up for a reason.

The next thing I knew, I felt an outpouring of light vibrations flowing through my being. I felt like I was receiving a download of raw data in the form of codes. I could not create a concept or story that I could grasp as it was information that was not currently in my human memory. Yet, I understood it clearly, on a deep subconscious level.

As with all my dream-visions, as soon as I attempt to insert my human, 3D brain, to make logical, structural, linear sense of what I am seeing, I shoot back into my body. It was wondrous to note that this new inner gateway remained available. It is a portal I can now traverse at will, a doorway to knowledge...

Your star lights the path

…we are each a star… a spray of beautiful lights shooting from our core… no two alike… differing colours, lengths, densities… jagged and smooth… ripples and points…

There was a news media clip about an astrophysicist mapping the human cells of a cancer patient with his star-gazing telescope equipment. The image on the computer screen appeared to be a night sky full of twinkling stars. As the telescope retracted its view these little starry lights clumped together to became cells. As the telescope retracted further, these cells become a solid mass, as we believe our bodies to be.

In reality, we are a collection of photonic lights even though we cannot physically feel or see them without a telescope. This is how we are structured beneath the denseness of our skin suits. We are stardust that is in constant motion.

These lights expand as waves and tentacle-like rays all around us. This star is our very own unique light signature. Ascension of consciousness is all about expansion. To ascend our consciousness, we expand our light rays to connect further and further outwards. These tap into vortices and portals that feed us the eternal endlessness of our potential.

These portals are doorways that funnel knowledge and information to us. It is through these portals that blueprints for new, previously unimaginable ideas, technologies, thoughtforms, philosophies and systems come to us. The greater number of feeder points we have open and accessible, the more information we are able to access; therefore, the greater and more expanded our perspective.

In our Soul-human skinsuit, our Light taps a vast repository of information to assist us to evolve fully past our primitive, animalistic natures. Some feed our physical requirements, some our mental or spiritual. Some feed our Soul. One of these doorways leads to the great library of all that our Soul has ever been or ever experienced. All of its gifts, talents, skills and knowledge since its beginning are present there.

Through some of these portals we process what we need for our own expansion. Through others we simply allow the Light to enter and flow through us to wherever it is meant to go.

In reality, we are a collection of photonic lights even though we cannot physically feel or see them without a telescope.

The pulse of creation stimulates this illumination within us. The key is to allow the boundless infinity of this energy to flow out from our core as far as it will reach. The more we build it up, the more it flows with fluidity and flexibility. When we erase thoughts of a perimeter, such as dogmas, rules, should be's, can't be's and must be's, the Light regains its flexibility and can be shaped and directed.

As we perceive what this knowledge, pulled through dimensions, can do for ourselves and all humankind, we will find a type of freedom never before experienced.

I dreamed of a nurse...

From the scenes taking place all around her it appeared to be wartime and from the clothing it appeared to be the First World War. She was in a hospital surrounded by many, many wounded and dying. The hospital was overflowing, the staff was overtaxed, supplies were increasingly limited. I sensed it was a desperate situation and they were unable to fully relieve the pain and suffering around them.

The woman was a junior, very young, and very new to her job. The war had thrown her head-first into the fire, so to speak, without benefit of years of practice. She was suffering greatly on behalf of all those whom she tended.

She went about her tasks, never resting, seldom stopping, unfailing in her duty. She held hands, she soothed fevers, she administered medications and whatever else was required. She sat by bedsides, helped write notes to loved ones, she listened, she cried with them, and she held them as they passed away.

Yet, deep in herself, she felt useless compared to the more experienced nurses. She did not believe she was fulfilling a proper service and worse, that perhaps she was harming others due to her lack of experience.

There was a doctor-type figure in the dream. A friend to whom she confided her concerns in a weak moment. Perhaps she was not suited to this type of work after all and should leave. In a casual moment he mentioned this to a lady who seemed to be in charge.

Her response was totally unexpected. Contrary to what the young nurse may think, she was the best nurse they had, perhaps more so because she did not know this about herself.

The young one was a jewel. It was her great capacity to love that was more important than her inexperience. She truly loved. She freely and fully shared her love with each and every person she came into contact with.

Love heals. It carries the frequency of life, even into, and beyond, physical death.

You are the key

*…keeper of the flow… magic… the entrance
to a mystical alchemical journey…
lead is turned into gold…*

The heart that is opened to the Soul electrifies
and magnetizes. It pulses with Light in harmony
with Source. This pulsing ignites the forge of alchemy. Here the Soul-mind merge of our embryo
self rises through the physical to fully embody in
the human, until it climbs ultimately into the very
heart of our Source.

At this point, the next pathway opens. The pathway beyond unity. Here all is so intertwined,
merged so intimately, as to dissolve into one

another, to become one and the same. Here the Soul-human-Source is one entity. Here there is no concept of unity versus separation. There is no thought to differentiate or polarize. There is no need for rules, regulations, moral codes. All is *in* all. The human-Soul is so enmeshed with the Light of Source as to *be* it. Breaking away from it is like a death, never to be contemplated.

Our human body and our Soul have a symbiotic relationship. This is one of the greatest partnerships of a Soul's long existence.

We are a member of large tribes of humans, other animals, insects, fish, birds, vegetation, all sentient beings, a vast seething complex of life that we call Earth. It is to this complex of life that we are married, that we are tied, and that we are obligated. We must cultivate the strength of this connection and make sense of it.

The magic of this connection is what enhances our spiritual resources. Without understanding the absolute necessity of this connection, we are not wholly human, we have not served our purpose here, and we have disappointed our Soul's intent in coming here.

Our human body and our Soul have a symbiotic relationship. This is one of the greatest partnerships of a Soul's long existence.

Our Soul is our anchor. The Soul in its cosmic dwelling place cannot experience the sensory. It cannot fully assimilate its understandings without the sensory experience of a human form and the playing field of free will choice. Its intent is very simple; to prompt us to do only what is best for us in order to have these experiences. Throughout our life it continually prompts, hoping we choose to listen.

What you will experience is something like a voice emanating from our Soul. It dialogues with us in every moment we breathe, from birth to death. Our Soul talks with us in a manner to which we alone will respond, and its prompts are never unkind or negative.

It communicates through the physical sensations of our body, skin responses such as shivers, goose bumps, heat or cold, muscle spasms, a pain or tightening here or there. Also, through dream images while sleeping or awake, or a voice sounding from deep within the area of our solar plexus, and much more. Deciphering the unique and personal meaning of these responses allows a clear direction to our actions and exploring this can be a fascinating journey.

Our Soul is also the conduit for the Light-love that reaches out to us from our Source. As we stabilize the connection with our Soul we partake of the miraculous sensation of the love-Light flowing from our Source, our Creator, to us. As all of that work comes to fruition and infuses every microscopic level of our being, there is one more task.

As above, so below and also within. The trans-
mutation of fear to love. By transmuting every
molecule of our being, we are able to fly free from
this earth dimension of entrapment to our natural place in the loops of infinite creation flowing
out from Source and returning to Source. Earth's
cycle of incarnations is a detour, not the Soul's life
sentence.

Our heart is our bridge. Between heaven and
earth. Between the creator and its creations. We
are the keepers of the Light. Our heart is the
keeper of the flow where Source Light and the
human mind-will axis converge.

Our heart is a diamond prism, attracting and
projecting infinite combinations made from the
Light of Source's delight, its love for its creations.
Within its vast caverns we do our most important
work. It is hidden work, yet it is the reason that
we have taken on a human form. It is our end of
the infinity loop.

The heart is an exchange terminal. At times, the exchange is passive. For example, we feel compelled to show up somewhere, without understanding why. There we engage in a seemingly random way. Flows of grace are exchanged without us realizing. At times it is an active exchange. We are guided to direct the flows of grace, as healers, teachers, guides, mentors.

Our heart is our bridge.

I was in an airplane...

I was jammed into economy, the plane packed to the ceiling with people and luggage.

I was on my way home from Italy, where I had just completed the second spiritual retreat of my life. It was a six-day intensive combination of kundalini yoga, meditation, and training in a specific healing method. It had been one of the most awe-inspiring weeks of my life on so very many levels.

In addition to the disciplines, the training, the vortex of energy created by 300 like-minded Souls, we were hosted by the peaceful beauty of Assisi, the home of famous Saint Francis, a beloved friend to my Soul.

I was exhausted. I had worked really, really hard! These retreats are not all bliss and Light! When led by a master teacher, however, the learnings infuse our being by the time we are ready to return to daily life.

Thus, I found myself suspended at 33,000 feet above the earth, floating in a state of oneness. This was my first experience of this state of just being. No projecting, no manifesting, no racing brain, no labels of status, job, name, gender. I had no fear, no emptiness within.

I was not truly aware of this until someone tapped lightly on my shoulder. It seems the flight attendant had been trying to get my attention. She was standing right beside me. I saw her there, I heard her voice and I heard her say my name, but I did not recognize the name as something belonging to me.

Finally, my travel companion had to tap me on the shoulder and I clearly remember looking up and thinking, "Oh, were you talking to me?"

If I had been able to separate myself to observe, I would have thought I was in the midst of a truly mind-blowing experience. But I was not in separation, I was in oneness and therefore it felt simply right.

I was detached from the stories I tell myself are my identity. I was fully in my body, merged in the sphere of my Soul and my Light.

Simply a soul in a human suit.

Awaken to your infinite dance

… awaken… mind and Soul…
whimsy and reason… infinite, multi-structured …

The span of our human life is a blip in the infinite timeline of our Soul. Significant, but a blip, nonetheless. Our Soul plays in dimensions we cannot perceive. Our one goal, perhaps above all others, is to awaken to the awareness of what we really are.

We think of and define ourselves as a physical human. Our human body and mind are everything to us and our Soul is possibly an add-on, if it exists at all. The focus of this view of reality is one hundred percent on the activity of our human survival and pleasures.

There is nothing mystical about being a spiritually conscious human.

Flip the perspective to view reality as one hundred percent Soul focussed. Imagine your Soul making a decision to come to this Earth planet to merge with a carbon-based life-form. In this Soul-first version we would find ourselves more concerned with how our Soul is managing here, than with how our body and mind are doing. We would want to know different things, such as *why* our Soul came here, *how* we can meet its objectives and *when* can we return to our Soul's home.

To 'know thyself' is to know that we are spirit, soul, energy, photonic lights, vibratory frequency, constant motion, existing in a carbon-based skin suit. To awaken is to become aware of each of these layers and their needs. To do this we need to develop an alternate way of sensing and understanding, a refining of the way we perceive.

Raising our consciousness is really refining our consciousness. To refine something means moving it from the gross to the fine, like taking large chunks of rocks and processing them to tiny grains of sand. In human terms, from large, macro-motor skills to the development of the fine, micro-sensory skills.

There is nothing mystical about being a spiritually conscious human. The skills needing to be refined are the senses we have held dormant for thousands of years. Those that lie beyond our five gross senses of taste, smell, hearing, touch and sight in the intricate nuances of our inner planes. When we search in the depths of our hearts, we discover deeper and deeper layers of seeing, hearing, feeling, until our inner planes spring fully multi-dimensionally alive. We use our inner senses to perceive the multi-dimensional layers of our external world. Events viewed by our external perception as right or wrong, black or white, may show on the inner plane as having three, four, five, or more layers of less tangible meaning. What appears solid physically, shows itself to have tightly interwoven layers of light and frequency.

Refining really means expanding beyond our current perceptions. Allowing this expansion propels our minds into areas of imagining hitherto unbelievable. When we release the belief that our exploration of thought has a boundary, we are faced with unheard of concepts that may be potentially scary to our ingrained mental controls. These stretch the boundaries of our knowledge like an infinite balloon inflating around us. The tightly woven layers of the physical around us loosen until we see each layer is constructed of infinite numbers of even finer layers woven or layered together.

On many levels, we can look at human history as a series of time frames cued to help us understand that it is possible to exist in human form as well as thrive in our spiritual consciousness. Throughout the ages, great teachers have planted seeds to aid us. For our part, it is an eons-long journey of self-awareness.

At all times, we have vast amounts of knowledge and information at our fingertips, or more precisely at the ready within our Soul, to enable a forward leap should we choose it.

I dreamed of a woman...

She stood high on a table-top mesa. She was tall, stately, composed. Her robes were those of an ancient priestess, yet she was fully human.

The air was still. Nothing was moving. She was barely breathing.

The mesa was dried and reddish in colour. The sky above was an indistinct grey-blue. There were no creatures or plants. It was like a desert, yet it felt cold and I shivered in my sleep.

She was looking down, far, far down. Below in the valley there were villages. People moved to and fro about their business. Dogs barked, sheep and goats bleated. There were people of all ages and skin colours. All mingling together tending to their daily tasks.

It was an overwhelming bustle of activity for this woman. Children, adults, pets, shops, and farms. Yet she was watching keenly. Her thoughts seething.

A part of her enjoyed a sense of superiority, high above the rest of humanity, even as this gave her deep pain. She was fearful to go among them because they caused her pain. She was angry because they caused her pain. Self-inflicted pain.

She was beautiful, yet so cold and aloof, blocking her vast reservoir of power, causing it to seethe within like a raging furnace with no outlet. This pain she held was like fire that builds and builds into a conflagration she cannot control.

It escapes through her hands with each gesture, and through her eyes with each glance. Her pain and anger folds in on itself, blinds her, burns her, until she separates from her Soul.

There was a soft voice calling to her from a place deep within, as a mother would call to a beloved child. It told her that fear and pain are of no account, they are illusions. She was caught in a predictive cycle. She was being careless with her Light.

By withholding her Light, she created chatter in her mind against these people, and this created pain in her heart.

All it would take was to move one foot forward and begin the walk down from the cliff. All it would take was one touch to another Soul and the pain would transform to love and the Light would flow.

Yet still she stood, anchored to the cliff edge.

I woke in deep sadness, thinking…when and why did we allow terror to replace love…

Allow the primal beat
of your heart

allow... layer upon layer upon layer...
endless expansion... as one breath dissipates
another takes its place...

Arguably one of our greatest gifts is the ability to dream, to imagine the unimaginable. These flights of whimsy never leave our memory. It is like pouring blue liquid into clear water. The colors merge to an equalization. The water is no longer clear or blue, but a different colour created from both, as well as an expanded volume.

Our mind expands by grasping, imagining, creating new ideas. It sorts through these using our personal and collective memories and understandings.

Trying or allowing. Trying is an active process, one that constricts energy into a pre-defined set of parameters. It is the projective polarity. When projecting, all incoming frequencies are blocked by the outward flow.

Allowing is a passive process, one of relaxation which removes restrictions. It is the receptive polarity. It opens to allow whatever is to come the freedom to unfold.

It is our gift and our responsibility to allow each person's version of reality to exist undisturbed, to allow each their free choice to move, shift or change.

Allowing makes room in our mind to open doors to the unimaginable. What we believe creates our reality. Constricting the ramblings of the imagination creates a restrictive reality. Our Earth is far more than one reality into which we all are to mold ourselves. In the laws of our multi-dimensional universe, all of our realities are allowed to exist at the same time.

There is no limit to the holographic nature of the energy fields around us, in the space we think is empty. Our 3-dimensional world exists within, and as a part of, all other dimensions. Infinite numbers of realities are taking place all around us.

It is our gift and our responsibility to allow each person's version of reality to exist undisturbed, to allow each their free choice to move, shift or change. If a person chooses a reality that is harmful to themselves or others, that is their sovereign responsibility. If harm spills into the greater tribe then the intent of their Soul is not being honored, for the intent of the Soul is to forge its own path but do no harm.

Our multi-dimensional existence asks for tolerance of others' reality without judging them to be right or wrong, or to conform or seek conversions by mind-control or force. This goes far beyond compassion. It is a whole new level of existence to one of total freedom of the individual to choose its own version of Soul-human existence.

In the human-Soul connection, we see beyond the veil of illusion that causes us to feel as a separate, cut-off fragment floating lost in space. To feel that our Soul is on the other side of the veil and our body is on this side of the veil.

When we bind together the frequencies of our human-Soul and open our connection to Source, we come to understand that this veil is an illusion that can be blown away in a puff. We allow all to simply be.

I dreamed I was speaking with my cells...

Yes, the tiny cells that make up every part of my body. It seemed strange even in my dream state.

They were little starry points of light. As I watched them more intently several came closer and bounced around me in a strange little dance. They were moving around me like tiny little beings. I was finding much humor and delight in watching them, wondering what this was all about.

Suddenly they stopped dancing and began waving desperately at me. When they had my very focussed attention, they spoke:

"We are you" … well, yes, of course, that made sense … "and we're dying in here" … well, that was a little more disturbing.

They began to dance with increasing agitation around me.

"You are ignoring us as if we do not exist." … well, yes, I did understand that too, but still could not figure out the problem or the urgency.

An image appeared to help me understand. In it, I was turning away from my child and stating, "I no longer know you. You were never mine. I have no interest in you."

They spoke directly to me again: "We are you. There is no separateness. What you are, we are. You created us as we are."

Ah… finally, I think I understood…

Fractals upon fractals

...fractals... mind, heart,
will... fractals upon fractals...
points on a fractal tree... the spaces between...

The space between everything is not empty. While we may not have determined exactly what it is made of, we know it is a conduit.

Imagine the web of consciousness as a geometric fractal pattern that never ends, yet is rooted in the originating point, which is Source. We are an extension of this original root, and we can trace our way back to it through the fractal latticework.

We are one emanation of the One Source. Every living creature is a fractal of this emanation. We are connected forever to it, and to all others through this fractal network of energy. The power of the One finds our hearts through this great branching mechanism.

All of our belief systems, traditions, lifestyles, societal structures, are like a great branching tree, a fractal network. Each new layer of understanding creates an expansion of Self and a greater comprehension of the Whole. Each understanding is an added layer that opens up our view to cosmic proportion. It provides a sense of the greater creation humming all around us. We are one part of this ever-growing fractal-tree of cosmic Souls.

Our body is our Soul. Our Soul is our body. Our cells are our responses to our Soul. They are the end result of our manifestation-creations. They are perfect because we have created them. In whatever its shape, our body is a manifestation of the image we have projected and commanded to take form.

When we look in a mirror and declare from our heart that our image is lumpy, the cells organize themselves to be lumpy. The body is an animation of our mind's projection. It can be re-animated or de-animated. As the Soul manifests its experiences on a macro level, the body and the cells respond on a micro level. To master the process of manifestation is to master the macro and the micro, on all levels from spirit to material.

Fractals upon fractals. Growing multi-dimensionally in all directions simultaneously. We can stick our hand into a ripple of water and the ripple shifts in direction, or size, but it does not stop rippling until its natural energy has been expended.

There are powerful currents running through every molecule of our earth. We are both a contributor to and the end result of these. The multiple crossing points of our creations intersect and overlap, compounding in a massive rhythmic wave. We contribute individually and collectively, both here and through all dimensions as these waves dance around and interact with the growth of other fractal networks. We are indivisible from the Whole.

The connection to the Light of our Source gives us unlimited power to create what we want to experience here, and to avoid creating what we do not want to experience.

We are taught from a young age how to exercise the tools in our minds. We seek with our mind. We began to seek at the moment of our first breath. We find what we seek through expressions of the heart. This process never ceases. At a certain point we seek outside our Self for answers in the collective. The extent to which we seek is a result of our personal capacity for flexibility.

When we are taught to think on only one track to the exclusion of all others, a line has been crossed. This is interferance in the natural flow of creative movement. By creating a person's reality for them through imposition, we are ultimately creating harm to them, and harm to every other dimension of the fractal growth linked to both them and us.

The connection to the Light of our Source gives us unlimited power to create what we want to experience here, and to avoid creating what we do not want to experience. The only end to this seeking is when our mind says, "Enough!" At this point fractal growth stops. The flow of Creation is dammed up, like stopping the flow of an immense river.

Creation is continuous movement. If we pause and focus on one fractal branch alone, the movement of creative growth follows in that direction. As it manifests it will create its own fractals and its own entanglements and fractal growths. We do not need to understand what those will be. In other words, we do not always need to know the outcomes.

We only need to believe our part is creating something that is both essential and intentional.

I dreamed of a monk...

He was a lovely monk. He radiated kindness, grace, Light. His eyes were as innocent as a child, yet ancient in wisdom and rich in depths I longed to reach. I wanted to stay with him forever, in whatever place he lived.

For surely that place would teach me to vibrate with his same grace and Light. What more could I want in this life than to exist in such bliss?

One moment he was there and the next moment my vision became cloudy.

Then suddenly - I split into two.

One of my selves morphed into a vivacious, beautiful young woman. She had long, flowing blond locks, colourful clothes, and a fancy convertible car. She was laughing and joking and having an excellent time – with no one in particular, it seemed.

She jumped into the car and sped off to attend a wedding. I noticed that she was driving over a frozen lake, over very thin ice, which did not seem to bother her at all. Over it she flew, disappearing into the distance, her joyful voice echoing on the wind.

At that point, the other half of me turned serenely to the lovely monk as if to say, "Okay, she is gone and she is happy, now can we go inside and begin."

The monk opened a gate and we entered a sanctuary teeming with life. There were flowers in all colours, birds of all varieties, lovely benches upon which to meditate, a beautiful stone building off in the distance. I felt I had come home and could live quietly here with my Soul the rest of my days.

We were greeted by a man who appeared to be the head of the place. I was drawn to him immediately for he was aged and wise and his Soul called to mine.

But... he was startled to see me. This unsettled me greatly.

He gently explained that I did not have to make a choice. I did not have to split myself in two. There was no need to be cloistered to enjoy the bliss of the spirit. The spiritual and the human sides of our existence are fashioned to coexist in harmony.

He looked intently in my eyes for a long minute, nodded his head as if to confirm some unspoken message, and then kindly shooed me back the way I had come.

With a final loving glance, I turned and walked out into the sunlight...

Mirrors within mirrors

… you, me, Soul, Earth… mirrors and light…
truth and fiction… infinite connections…

We are mirrors within mirrors. Each new fractal is also a mirror. Each mirror creates a new branch.

We will never fully recognize the face in the mirror because it is only the shell of our current incarnation. It is not truly *us*. It is the skin suit we wear over our Soul. The Soul is large, and it is within and without the body. It, too, has fractal fragments that come and go.

Our Creator-Source has given us a mirror to see with. The Creator's delight, his/her love for us which we know as Light, illuminates the mirror showing us the beauty abiding within every heart.

Our Soul holds this mirror up to our human self, to reflect us back to ourselves. It guides us in our interior life to our greatest love, far beyond the intellect.

A grace-filled heart calls us to be in concert with the elements around us and to put aside all things that would destroy or prevent that harmony.

A clear mirror reflects us back to ourselves. Turn the mirror and it reflects ourselves out to others. What we cultivate in our hearts is also an act of creation. The laws that govern that act of creating can never be changed. Once put in motion, they play out according to their properties. This creation will alchemically enter our surrounding field.

It is safe to say that we are not alone in this cosmos. The signs are endless and in plain sight for those with 'eyes' to see. Just because we cannot see clearly into these dimensions does not mean we are not impacting them. Exploding the atom bomb, as an example, has most likely created tremendous unimaginable harm in other dimensions around us. Just because we know how to do something does not mean we must do it.

We will always need systems to grow food, make implements, and create structures to maintain harmony when large groups live together. We can look out at our external world from within our Soul and apply our free will to choose what we will create and wish to see in the mirror of ourselves and our world.

Each individual's essence is to be sustained in the structuring of these to allow the web to grow stronger. The success of these systems lies not on what we do, but rather in the essence we infuse into how we do them. As each of us acts more and more often from the Light, there is a greater and greater outpouring of grace.

A grace-filled heart calls us to be in concert with the elements around us and to put aside all things that would destroy or prevent that harmony.

I dreamed of a water bearer...

She was graceful, supple and strong. There was an urn balanced effortlessly as an extension of her arms. She looked intently at me and said, "Listen."

"My urn is a vessel that stands ready. It is a storehouse of elements, all contained within its life-giving waters. These waters are neither to gush forth continuously, nor stop up completely, but rather are ready for use in appropriate amounts at appropriate times.

Water is the supreme element of flexibility. It seeks the path of least resistance, but always flows relentlessly towards something. It has the power to cleanse and soothe, lightening and purifying whatever it touches.

It is an unstoppable force of a magnitude that can change the face of the earth, through storms and floods. It is the little guy who confronts the giant. It can grow one droplet at a time to a great tidal motion of relentless force."

Her words brought to mind images of the love we humans have for water – waterfront homes, water parks where we splash like children, lakes and oceans where we feel the pull of tide and time, backyard pools, luxurious showers and baths.

On a subconscious level we come away from these treats feeling lighter, purer, freer as the 'debris' stuck to us has washed away. We can begin afresh.

Our body and blood are water. Water generates our power, and lack of it drains our life away. The water-bearer fills the urn of the heart and pours it out over all, in needed measure, in continuous love.

She said: "I see you as you take sanctuary in my grace and allow it to protect you. Let me be your vessel in this world, a channel for blessing. Hold tight to my urn and we will pour. Together we will power a torrent of divine treasure to the ends of the earth."

Your slumbering power

…power… unlimited, free…
slumbering within… mesmerizing,
hypnotizing… waiting to be claimed…

The Light of Source burns as a fire in a vast forge within every one of us. It is a unified field of energy that, by its unification, is an unstoppable force. Our human skin suits are built for power manifestation through the mind-heart-will axis. Our choice is how to manage all this.

Our power is bound only by the limits of our perception. The faster we release our perception of limit and lack, the greater our power to create.

Our beliefs are the key to releasing limitations to access this power source.

Power is the capacity to manifest something through alignment of the mind and the will in the heart. By this definition, we all have the same potential amount of power. We all have the capacity to manifest anything. The purity of our passion for our journey to find and fulfill our highest potential creates massive amounts of energy that spin within us. This gathers a huge force around us.

The power to manifest has no moral compass that attributes good or bad, light or dark. Reward and punishment are human-made morality. The natural laws of our universe simply create actions and results follow. We humans assign labels of good or bad. Our personal timeline is where we play out the consequence of actions we have set in motion. The actions we choose become the life events we will experience.

Power is a concept that we tend to equate to the rich, the famous, the higher-ups in our hierarchical systems, the priests and shamans. We say things like, "He is powerful, be careful, do not cross him. There are powerful undercurrents running there. She has more power than I do. That was a powerful storm. He is powerfully angry. She radiates power."

We have the sense that power is something great and vast, awe-inspiring and often potentially dangerous. We might even believe subconsciously that we must steer clear of power as we are not worthy of wielding it, or we might not do it right, after all, we are tiny humans compared to the titans of history.

When we believe we have no power of our own, we latch on to someone who we believe has it or has more of it. We think this makes us powerful by association. We think it fills an inner personal vacuum. Others know better, so we follow them or emulate them, and we will acquire the power they have. Surely, this power must also be ours to have.

*When we are guided by the vast power
of Light entering our heart,
we live bathed in grace.*

Power is not about who has special dispensations, privileges, or deserves it. Though many of our relationships can be attributed to this. Friends, colleagues, gurus, teachers. This type of thinking binds our power and keeps us from building capacity. We cannot contract out our spiritual work. It is ours alone to do.

We build a powerful capacity to manifest through the practice of holding a stable sensitive space in our hearts. The qualities of the space we hold is what will manifest. The greatest power in the cosmos is the intelligence field of the Source, that creates all. A tiny spark of this force is gifted to us to breathe life into our human bodies and remains active to maintain our life. Through this spark we have access to the vastness of Source's intelligence field.

We call this spark of life the Light, Light-Love, or Divine Love, and many other terms, but however we name it, it is our personal access point to the field of creation energy that powers the universe. We can access this cosmic force of Light by delving deep within the recesses of our heart space, where our Soul will provide a supply on demand. We couple that divine intelligence field with our hearts desire (our love) for a particular thing to be manifested. We then tether that to the strength of our human will and the tools within our mind. When these connect in perfect unified purpose there is an unstoppable force created through which we can manifest the desired element that began the process.

We do not need to look for this power elsewhere or in the interpretations of others. We are taught to conform to societal rules even when this gives the power of our internal knowing to an external authority. We are taught that a Soul is a thing we cannot understand, therefore we must look to experts for guidance.

When these things, our Soul and our humanness are taken from us, there is no replacement to anchor our inner Self. We feel some major part of our Self is missing. We seek outside, but we do not know what we seek. This is a classic form of control and dominance that renders us powerless.

We can do this dance forever. We can also choose to not do it. We can continue to unconsciously react to other's patterns, like driving to the store and responding to traffic patterns. Or we can consciously create the traffic patterns we want by focusing on bringing back our power within. I know this may seem hard to believe, but we can manifest our own required traffic patterns. This goes beyond intent and motive. This is another dimensional matrix that we can access.

We have become a planet of fear because we have subconsciously latched on to this matrix of external control. Deep within our Self, it builds from the collective beliefs layered over thousands of years. Our power spills out because we do not understand that we have it. Fear spews forth unchecked, the unconscious underlying current for our actions. It hits the convergence field and bounces back to all others in a wave more powerful than that we sent out.

This is what is meant by 'unleashing' a storm, a tempest. Once unleashed this energy of fear takes on a life of its own. Thus, fear becomes an entity that lives and breathes and feeds itself as it moves. It is the collective result of our inability to take personal responsibility for our power.

To express, to not express. We talk of casting spells as if it were something done by the ancients. Yet, we are all spellcasters, all the time. Through our speech, the timbre of our voice, through the use of specific words and rhythms, through our hand movements, body movements, and through the infinite combinations of all these that are exponentially stronger as a sum total. This is a power that can be used for control and dominance or for compassion, empathy, sympathy, and mercy.

We have become a planet of humans who express at the emotional level almost all the time. Crying, laughing, the fire of our anger. Emotion is a release process that is essential. It is the process through which we release the built-up energy of deeply felt events. A process whereby we manifest through the physical the depth of our thoughts. Emotions are our steam valve. After the excess steam has been released, the next step is to expand our understanding, let the story content go, and return to a balanced equilibrium.

Without these steps, we get stuck in a cycle of emotional expression, reliving and repeating the same patterns over and over through different events. This cyclical pattern blocks the power within our hearts. The incoming Light gets stuck. Our power and stability are in the middle way, the neutral way, where we must return quickly from either extreme. Here the flow of Light naturally opens our grace.

When we are guided by the vast power of Light entering our heart, we live bathed in grace. Grace is like water. In this pool there is no need for rules, hierarchies, virtues, right or wrong, for we become a human manifestation of Light and Love. It is as a river allowed its natural course through rocks, sand, whirlpools, creeks, and oceans. It is always in harmony with itself, knowing that around the next bend it will require a different flow.

I dreamed of a panther...

It was sleek and black and ancient. It was also impatient and nudged me imperiously to leap onto its back. It took off so quickly it took all my strength to hang on. It transported us deep into the rocky foundations of the Earth.

We were in the depths of a cave. There was no light, and it was eerily silent. It unceremoniously dumped me off its back and flopped down a little distance away. It stared at me as if to say, "You should know this, I should not have had to bring you here."

I was trembling, waiting. Suddenly, there it was – or, rather, there they were.

Spiders. Thousands of spiders in all shapes and all sizes. They caught sight of me, they advanced upon me, they crawled all over me and covered me from head to foot. I was paralyzed with fear, barely breathing.

But... they just sat there. They did not move, did not bite, did not spin their webs around me. They simply clung to me and stared at me expectantly. We eyeballed each other for what seemed ages. What on earth was I supposed to understand from all this?

I was suffocating. In desperation, I called to Panther to help. His eyes glowed bright yellow and then I knew.

These spiders trapping me were themselves trapped. Stalemate. Oh, the webs we weave. Such a famously trite phrase. I was entrapping them by my actions and by these actions, they were being entrapped. Do we understand that the webs we weave, the people we catch in them, the circumstances we cre-

ate by them, are themselves caught and wishing to leave us?

Mmm... I began freeing these spiders one at a time and they happily scurried away. Finally, there was one left. A huge black widow covered my entire back and shoulders. I reached behind and gently dislodged her. She came easily around to my front and settled low on my gut. We locked eyes and there was a flow of unspoken messages between us.

"The unconscious beliefs that foster fear, entrapment, separation weave the tightest webs around you – are all connected to you. Let these go, free the memories. You know your true Self. Free the binding and you free more than just yourself."

A matrix awaits

…wheels within wheels… seeds… matrix…
old ways, new ways… what we believe,
the space we hold…

Light feeds grace into the convergence field and the field, therefore, returns grace to us and every other living thing. Grace seeds grace. The matrix shifts.

Each choice we make opens up possibilities and potentialities. Each reveals a different set of coordinates on the grid, which unleashes a new set of possible directions to move. This becomes an entirely new matrix grid of coordinates. Each matrix is a never-ending fractal tree of potential.

We live in a matrix of energy fields. Science calls it *quantum entangled frequencies*. Spiritualists call it ether. Religions call it heaven and hell.

One matrix lives within another, which lives within another, and another and another. Think of it as wheels within wheels containing choices within choices that open us to different matrices of possibility, potential, and experience.

Our choices can take us in any direction, for our good or for our detriment. Into life as a free Soul-human, or into further entrapment.

We can no longer ask for forgiveness on the grounds that we know not what we do. We are in an age where so many matrices are visible. Those we have been living in for thousands of years are now clearly perceptible. New and different matrices are also visible, giving us other choices never before known to us. To find them we must transcend our collective memories and allow for the unknown to catalyze our minds and personal will. There is also a fresh resonance deep within many, asking to look, sense, hear, and feel through different methods.

We make our choices from the material we have stored in our memory bank of experiences. We cannot perceive or comprehend a choice that lies outside these parameters. Most of what we view as choice in our lives, is not truly a free choice, it is an extraction from what we already perceive within our memory.

As a result, we are trapped in a matrix with concise boundaries and parameters. Yet these are created by our *own* memory, which in turn was created by collective experience over time. This is the boundary of our reality.

When we shift the matrix within us away from our stored memory, it automatically, and instantly, recalibrates our external reality. *In* one is *in* the Whole. The sensation of these new realities must be seeded into the matrix of the Whole to become real. Someone must be the first to grasp and live an unknown concept. It then becomes accessible to all through the web.

New threads are created and grown by consistent seeding of this type. To extract ourselves from one matrix of beliefs in order to move to another feels like banishment from all that we are comfortable with. Yet, comfort does not equate to good.

The current reality matrix that is most persistent, and perpetuated, is one of entrapment through fear. It is peddled to us as beneficent hierarchical systems that coerce us to bow to external dominance. The wolf in sheep's clothing. Coercion by comfort. The world is as it is because our collective beliefs are hard with judgment, rage and grief. Thus, our world is hard-wired to a matrix of fear and retribution.

Our myths and history fill us with stories of vengeful gods, wars, destruction and self-righteous behaviours, often in the name of transcendence – or the right of the "right" to win above all. We feed our children these stories from their birth, even in our lullabies, which trains them to believe this matrix of fear and judgement is the truth of our world.

It may appear on the surface that it is impossible to get out of this web. Fear adds power to shadows. It creates shadows where there are none to begin with. Our memory is a massive holder of past images and often works against us. We are so embedded in the current matrix that it is a major leap to imagine anything different. We cannot see the forest for the trees. Rather, we are afraid to walk far enough away from the trees to see the forest.

The logical, linear part of our mind creates identity through labels, the mirror of others, memories, objects, jobs, relationships. It cannot comprehend that all of these are merely facets, like pieces of a ballroom mirror ball, of our unified Self. We place our deepest fears and hopes, and those fragments of the Self that we have created here in our human form, in identities that we perceive as far away from us - in other dimensions, in past lives, the spirit worlds, in a hell, heaven or purgatory.

Recalling all of these fragments to ourselves is a necessary undertaking to become a unified Soul-human. It is a crucial process, because most of our Soul is outside this human dimension, looking in on us, urgently trying to retrieve the parts of us which are stuck inside this repetitive reality of Earth incarnations.

Our collective reality is created from a historical platform of thought, experience, and belief that has repeated and augmented generation to generation. This content is currently shifting at a rapid rate as new knowledge is being discovered and disclosed in vast amounts every year.

Major attempts are being made to fix the current matrix by making slight shifts to it. This is an attempt to re-form a new matrix out of the broken webs of the old. A difficult task for even the most robust of spiders! Yet it is not working, and, arguably, we are worse off than before and we are killing our planet in the process.

*We can no longer ask for forgiveness
on the grounds that we know not
what we do.*

We tend to focus on understanding the building blocks of this matrix in more depth, to learn how to work with it more efficiently. This is why our global governments and economies spin in repetitive cycles. We can either cling to our old ways of understanding as they are disproved and disintegrate, or we can step into the new and look around in wonder to see where this will lead us.

The correction in perception lies outside of the old. The old matrix is like an experiment gone awry and is consistently taking us down the rabbit hole of perceived separation from our Self and our Source. We can back out of that hole with a little effort. Freedom from the binding laws of entrapment and fear is found outside this old matrix, quixotically found deep inside our own Self. We need to leap to our inner dimensions to develop a new way of believing and being.

We cannot change the laws of a matrix when we are in them. We can, however, transcend them. We can re-write this program one individual at a time. It is the individual that will shift the collective, not the other way around. We are too far into the societal structure that has been created over thousands of years, to unravel it through the group. The more power we invest in this group collective, the more power it holds to keep us tied.

To transcend this reality, we must call in the sensation of the new reality we want to have and hold it steadily in the quiet sensitive space of our heart. We then release all memories, stories we tell ourselves, or labels we attach to ourselves that do not carry the frequency of this new matrix.

The new matrix to take us out of entrapment and fear is found by following the heart's inner path through our Soul to the Light of Source. Here all separation and polarization, fear, helplessness and entrapment disintegrate, then dissolve, as if they never existed.

It may seem hard, but it is possible to let go of the old way of existing. The new way of manifestation through the heart's Light creates a world of grace and freedom. Where we live *in* the Soul, not from the Soul. A walking Soul. A Soul on legs.

One aspect of the spiders in the dream represented the labels and stories I tell myself are my Self. I call myself a mother, because I have children. Unconsciously I shoulder a host of mother-defining expectations.

In reality, I am simply a Soul existing in a single moment in time. I can live within the matrix of motherhood that carries all manner of inherited dictates to be, think and do in relation to a child, a matrix that separates the unified Whole of oneness into segments, or I can live in a matrix of perfect love, carrying no labels, to be simply a Soul in action with another Soul. Meeting that Soul as an equal and at the state that Soul resides.

Each matrix has its set of laws created by all who input to it. These are binding. We are non-severable from with these laws, while we are still consciously and unconsciously contributing to them. Conscious and/or unconscious participation is the power that creates what we have in our matrix. Every time we say or think something like "oh my goodness, I am so afraid of the dark, I cannot walk in the woods at night" we are consciously weaving and binding the matrix of fear around ourselves.

Through the convergence field between all things, we are binding our fellow humans, as this matrix of fear bounces back and into everyone else. This seems rather a simplistic example, but the principle holds true for the more complex. Deep within our psyches are unconsciously held fears that bind us in the same manner.

We cannot change the laws of a matrix when we are in them. We can, however, transcend them.

Once we move our conscious participation to another matrix, we automatically create that new matrix. The new matrix will show us its new building blocks in order for us to fully release the bindings of the old. It is the inner path that leaps over the old external path. It literally leaves the old behind, does not even acknowledge the old as being relevant.

Creation equals participating consciously and knowingly. No one, no external authority, can ever command our inner space and, consequently, what we choose to create. This power is the greatest power there is. We live in the new while keeping our physical space in the old.

In the new matrix Love is our first response to everything. This first response permeates from the micro to the macro levels, to all our physical cells, through our energy fields, imbues every conscious and unconscious projection, such that the matrix of fear we left behind is no longer within us at any level. If we are contemplating for even a nano-second the choice of love over fear, consciously or unconsciously, we are still in a matrix of separation, with fear still haunting us at some level.

We leap to the new matrix through the great alchemy of the Soul-human-Light merge. It is not a linear leap such that we can say "aha, I leapt." Imagine it as moving from an outer wheel to an inner wheel. The grace-filled heart shifts gears, steps to the other matrix, holds greater expansion of Light, and allows the new building blocks to form. No words are required. It is done in silence. We listen, and we know.

To know is to be at a loss for words. Words are our attempt to describe what we know. Knowing is a frequency that pulses in our heart. We become a fully spiritualized human.

In the new matrix Love is our first response to everything.

I dreamed of a little child...

Its smiles, giggles, burbles, and lovely chubbiness held my attention. It spread love so effortlessly.

The scene shifted and I was at the beach. It was one of those days blessed with sun and warm breezes and calm ocean. Perfect for swimming, soaking, wiggling toes in the sand. I was walking, lost in the beauty, for I love ocean beaches above all other places.

A toddler ran into my path and planted himself in front of me. He plunked down his little pail and pulled his collection of rocks out for my inspection, one by one.

I gently touched his arm and his head. Unknowingly, it was a form of unspoken blessing. I felt a pulse go between us as I looked into his merry little eyes, eyes that had gone still, time stopped.

We smiled slowly at each other, and a wave of grace filled the air. That was it, one tiny moment, and off he ran to join his mother. I continued walking, back once again in my inner world.

The scene shifted again. This time I was in a quaint little restaurant. Another adorable toddler appeared in the arms of its parent. I carried my coffee and muffin in search of a free table. I noticed this child. I smiled slightly and continued to walk.

As I sat and arranged my food, there was a wave of disturbance swirling around the room. I looked up and what I saw was so lovely.

This angelic little child was smiling and laughing, attempting to leap from his parent's arms as he shared his joy with everyone. He was too young for words, yet he was commanding the attention of every guest, waving till they lifted their heads, holding eye contact with each until they smiled and laughed back.

He was beaming Light. All of us could feel the frequency shift within ourselves in response.

Soul seeking Soul.

Your wonder lights the unknown

... the wonder of the unknown...
creation's pulse... where will it go...
what will it do...
Source's delight as it observes itself in us...

Source's intelligence pulses out energetic expressions that never fully retract to the originating point. The outgoing expansion and contraction take on the principles of absorption and incorporation, rather than contraction and exclusion. Raw materials in an infinite state of possibility and potentiality. Through absorbing these we can revel in wonder.

Wonder is a spiritual technology.

Wonder is the replacement for why. Why is an intellectual inquiry that keeps us in our minds. Wonder opens us to possibilities we could never imagine. Wonder not only allows us to inquire intellectually, but also to dream of the possibilities beyond intellectual inquiry.

Wonder simultaneously opens the mind, the heart and the solar plexus, seat of our personal will. Wonder allows our mind to relax its functions of logic, reason, process, to float in the illuminating Light of our heart.

In wonder, we reflexively breathe in lifegiving energy and are transported to an altered reality, where we access the full power of our imagination. This frequency opens golden tunnels to other dimensions where we can absorb the unknown of never-before-imagined understandings, information, knowledge and allow the transfer of information back and forth.

Wonder is a spiritual technology. It allows our hearts to relax and fully open, to transcend the preconceived or predetermined. It grounds us in our heart. It tunes into our Soul, transcends thought, spins grace. Discipline is about shifting. Wonder shifts us to heart-centered Soul dialogue and the experience of our personal understanding of our unique Soul-human journey.

Wonder's discipline transports us into the dwelling place of our Source, the Creator, the One Unmanifest, Divine Intelligence. It teaches us to hold that Light in our hearts and allow grace to flow at all times, in all places and in all ways. To touch grace in a sensory, visceral way is to know its vastness, and its ability to transcend any elements that would pull us away from it.

We develop discipline of spirit for our own selves. When our Soul leaves our body to return to its home, it returns alone, and it answers alone. It speaks only for its own creations. Our earth journey is a fascinating one in that we are self-contained, a solitary Soul, and yet interdependent, on the human tribe, at the same time. We are intended to be unconditionally interdependent.

We have no real ability to place conditions on our fellows, though we may think we do. They too must stand self-contained and alone at their return home from this life. In a seeming paradox, once we individually shift our spiritual discipline to live in wonder, our Light catalyzes tribal interdependence as grace is shared upon all around us.

Our inner essence informs the motivation that makes the choice and decides the action. A wonder-infused understanding will create altered thought patterns, behaviors and actions. These will automatically have an effect on how we create our social systems and structures. As we allow wonder to tune us to the Light, we become so fundamentally altered by its frequency that all that is pulling apart our earth, water, skies, animals, plants, people will automatically cease.

The Light of Source shows us we are all originally one. Harm to others inflicts harm on ourselves. The sacredness of another is unquestioned.

I was in the grocery store...

I was minding my own business, pushing my cart, searching for some cheese in the cheese section. All of a sudden, I heard a voice behind me say, "Well, hello, long time no see."

It had been a decade since I left my corporate job. During that time my path had taken me far from those with whom I had worked, some of whom had been friends for a time. Yet, I recognized that voice instantly. I turned around and smiled a little tentatively.

This was a person whose one action decades previously had caused tremendous suffering in my life. In one of those strange circles of connections, this

person had said something to another person, caus-
ing the story of my life at that time to blow apart.

We had never discussed this between us, leaving
those actions to lie dormant and hopefully forgot-
ten, as simply one of those things, an indiscretion,
a misjudgment, a misplaced intention. My life had
carried on, the dust eventually settled over time,
and I ended up much better off than I was before.

I held no grudge against this person. Yet, in the
way of some memories, the details were unfaded
as part of the story of that time. Perhaps there was
also something in his memory that was unsettling,
for the strangest thing happened.

As I was speaking words to him, the usual pleas-
antries of life, the weather, retirement, the grand-
kids, simultaneously there was a voice within me
that said, "I forgive you."

This voice came up out of the core of me, my heart
space and shot out through my third eye, clear as a
bell, literally as I was speaking other words out of

my mouth about the weather. My human self and my Soul self were communicating at the same time!

I was, of course, looking in his eyes as I was speaking, and the wonder of it was that I saw a response from his Soul that sounded something like, "thank you." I felt a frequency shift in myself and in the air around us.

I had not seen this person in over a decade, and after this ten-minute conversation, I have not seen him again... and I know I never will...

Weave your grace

… weaving grace… the primal beat of a heart…
one in flow with the universe…
a Soul voice softly speaking...

To find grace, do not look for it. To experience grace, do not attempt to structure it. To know grace, do not expect it to appear.

The act of conception, the act of first heartbeat, the act of birth, the act of first breath, the act of Soul-human merge. These are acts of grace.

In the womb, our hearts are the first organ to form. Light fills up this vessel to fuel our growth. Then the brain forms, and other organs, and so on, and we become a physical human. Our Soul enters the heart and merges with our baby mind, a second act of grace.

Our first breath is a third act of grace. Air flows into our lungs in seconds to feed a vast network of cells in our tiny bodies. A new human-Soul brings forward a new seed of Light into our world. This life is a new opportunity to revise the stories of our past through a new matrix of connections. A new life brings a breath of eternal 'time' suspended in a state of purity. Sacred oneness.

Grace is the essence of Source in action. Like the spinning of a spider's silken thread, it spins out from our heart. We all contain a tiny seed essence of our Source that we call the Light. In the beginning we are balanced upon the foundation of this. It powers our Light.

Grace is the flow of cosmic energy. When all of the laws of the earth and the cosmos are flowing undisrupted and untampered with, all things will manifest and unmanifest in each's correct rhythm and time.

Grace is the magic carpet that all else rides upon. It streams forth from the Light-field of our hearts. As we choose to activate it, it empowers every area of our life. It opens our senses to awareness of the intangibles manifesting all around.

Grace powers a flood of inner knowing, yet it is indescribable. We use this word in every language of the world, yet there is no clear translation. Its essence is powerful beyond our comprehension. Believe in its power and watch as it activates around us. Be in wonder of what it creates.

Grace is not ours to keep. It belongs to all. We are taught it is something granted to us as needed, or if we are good. We might wish to keep it to ourselves and it will protect us. These are myths to be dispelled. Grace is not to be hoarded within, rather acknowledged as it passes through us to others.

We tap into it more often than we know. When we get to the 'end of our rope,' 'hit rock bottom,' we unconsciously release our obsessive control and say, "I give up." As we soften the rigidity of our minds we rest in our hearts. In this natural softening, grace automatically manifests, not only to us but to all.

A grace-filled heart softens the stories we build from the layers of belief that have become our manifesto of personal rights. It maintains its personal rights within the embrace of loving responsibility to all. It can maintain both the individual's rights as well as the collective's rights at the same time. In our world, the rights of the individual supersede the harm to the collective.

Do the rights of one country's government supersede the harm to the global collective of countries? Do the rights of humans supersede the rights of all living creatures and the planet? Do the rights of my liver supersede those of my lungs or stomach or spleen? Imbalance can lead to death.

A grace-filled heart helps us understand the meaning of oneness versus unity. Unity implies the merging of various individual and separate groups. Oneness has no subdivisions into separate groups and never will. It is one sovereign entity. In oneness, the collective and the individual are the same entity. Harm to one equals harm to the other. Harm can never even be imagined.

The simple nature of our Soul is to be open and responding in every moment, with whatever action the moment requires. There are moments when we are called upon to step up with courage, knowledge, and action, moments that call upon our inner crusader to spotlight an injustice, to encourage, or inspire. Do so from a grace-filled foundation.

We have a good mind so we use it, we calibrate the information we have, we engage actively in life and relationships, we state our case, take action to right a wrong, express a wide range of emotions, we must still critique, speak our truth, answer sincerely. If help is required, we give it without judgement. If a critique is required, we give it without debasement or shame. If concerns must be highlighted, we supply them without emotion. If encouragement is called for, we supply it with enthusiasm.

Grace takes action through an infinite nuance of ways, in whatever form is an appropriate response. At a macro level these are noticeable to us mostly as empathy, sympathy, compassion, and mercy.

Empathy is a mental discipline. One in which we choose to intellectually understand ourselves in the place of the other, their suffering, their emotions, their actions. We can momentarily visualize ourselves starving as an example, even if we have never lived through this, and ponder how that might affect us.

Sympathy is an expression of empathy through words that speak our understanding of the other's experience.

Compassion is an action resulting from empathy. It is the action of reaching out. After we have made the intellectual decision to empathize, compassion is the decision to actively assist in some physical way.

A grace-filled heart softens the stories we build from the layers of belief that have become our manifesto of personal rights.

Mercy is the result of all these. It is a granting of the micro-nuances of grace. It says, "I am one with you. What you are, I am also, and therefore I will open and let you in to my heart. For there, as you stand before me in whatever state you are, there also do I stand. What is in you is in me. How I respond enters you and returns to me. What is in me is in you."

At the intersection point with others, our open heart overflows with grace. Choose to keep an open heart, no matter what. Choose to invoke an understanding of that other person or situation.

Choose to respond on the spectrum of empathetic-merciful acceptance, no matter how difficult the circumstance.

We are being called to work at the level of Soul exploration, acceptance, embodiment, and integration. No longer is this a journey for mystics, sages, or adepts, but a call to the general population of humans.

Grace sets all of us free. The more grace pours out from us, the less harm we will need to reverse. In the synchronicities, complexities, similarities, patterns, twists and turns of events that we create as our life, there is beauty to be found. Beauty is grace. Grace is healing.

I dreamed, yet I did not...

I sensed I had awakened from a very deep sleep. I was suspended in time. It seemed my eyes were open, yet I was not sure. There were images spiraling in my vision. It was impossible for me to tell whether it was my inner vision or my external vision. All my energy was focused on this strange dance before me.

I saw two images, possibly three, possibly more, all twirling, spinning and dancing in front of my eyes. They moved like a brilliantly-colored kaleidoscope.

First, I saw an X-shaped cross. Then, from behind the X came an upright cross so there were eight points circling and flashing – the symbol of com-

pletion. These eight points then became loops like those we call infinity loops. Figure eights layering upon each other and expanding to resemble a flower with 12 petals.

Behind this appeared the six-sided symbol we call the flower of life.

These two symbols kept shifting and morphing from one to the other. One behind the other, then in front of the other. They were all in one spot, they never separated, they were joined, they were merged, flashing from one to the other, one on top of the other. Strange multi-dimensional movements.

The Cycle of Infinity and the Cycle of Life and Death. Symbols of creation moving within and around each other. As above, so below. As within, so without. Life is infinity... infinity is life...

A seal on your heart

… seal the heart… make a pact, a guarantee…
our heart lives for only one law…

We channel the greatest power in the universe. Source Light. We carry the greatest human element ever created. Our heart. It is a gateway. Set an unbreakable seal of magnetic power around the heart. This seal is as a gossamer thin veil that allows Light to seep through, love to expand within, and grace to pass outward.

When the heart carries the seal of the love of the Source, of the Light of the Creator, it resonates with a magnitude that continuously pours grace into the world. The Light is our tiny taste of a vast, unlimited, unbounded energy. Within the heart we can sense this vastness and when it touches us, our consciousness opens to insight and illumination.

A heart sealed in the Light of Source bestows complete freedom upon us.

The organic nature of our body will never deceive us. It will tell us where we have placed our attention. Unlock the shadow over the heart that worships the external, the act of giving our power into another's hands. The frequency held within our hearts elicits a response from every cell in our body, including our brain. The ability of our mind to expand beyond anything we could ever imagine is the result of the seal of Source Light over the heart.

Always search in the heart. When we feel dislocated, we have separated from our heart-space and we're wandering around in our head or in our emotions or in a part of our body where there is pain. The traps of our psyche catch us in a net and constrict our movement. If we feel constricted, we have separated from our heart's Light.

Stop thinking, stop emoting or feeling, breathe in and turn the focus inward. Stop paying attention to whatever is going on externally and follow the exhaled breath to the inside of the body. Focus on the heart space within the physical chest cavity and allow a glow of Light to form and expand there.

Whisper to your Soul for assistance and ask for the truth of this particular moment to show itself to you through the lens of Source's perfect Love and Oneness. With practice this becomes an instantaneous wave of motion, such that we can drop into the still heart space in a nano-second. The goal is, of course, to never leave this space, to live every breathe of every moment, every thought, every emotion, every action from this place.

A heart sealed in the Light of Source bestows complete freedom upon us. For a mind and will sealed in Source's love through the heart, no transgression or separation from this Light could ever ensue, no fear could ever hold us captive, no power of entrapment could bind our Soul.

I dreamed of a lady...

She was dressed in the long, flowing gown of an era long past. A time of massive stone castles and chivalrous knights.

The Lady was in a stone chapel. It was very ancient, small and cold as only a stone building can be. I marvelled that she was so at peace with herself as she added items to the altar and gave her thanks.

The scene kept shifting rapidly. Next, she was in a village, surrounded by people of all ages requesting her tinctures, her advice, sharing their stories. I could feel the great wave of love of these villagers had for her and her for them.

In the next scene, the lady was sitting in a great stone hall beside a roaring fire, sewing work in her hands and children playing happily at her feet.

In the next, she was at a place where the forest met the meadow. Her hands were moving in some sort of ceremony with herbs, plant. She was totally engrossed and focused on her task.

Behind her stood a knight in full armour. He was watchful of her and the surroundings, respectfully guarding her space, so she could fulfill her purpose.

In the final scene, the knight and his lady walked their land. At each corner they stopped. He faced away from her scanning the near and far horizons. She took the time she required, and he honored this wholly, with no impatience, no disbelief. He trusted. She trusted. When her rituals were complete, they both moved on.

It was a beautiful dream. Such serenity, peace, quiet joy. A time when all was in balance. The knight was honouring the work of his lady as equal to his own.

Each person had a path equal in value to another, be they villager or lord, child or adult. Simply respect, integrity, honesty and the richness of life that flows from the wonder of being free.

As if on cue, a Shining One appeared with a cute, chirpy little bluebird on its shoulder. "Remember this place, the sensations. Remember..."

I opened my eyes and for a brief moment, I felt a visceral echo of that place in my waking Self.

Freedom,
the undying dance

… choose the path… the undying dance…
light the unknown… freedom…

All are bound by the laws of creation - the human,
the Soul, the Soul-human partnership, life, death.
There are countless other living beings scattered
throughout the universe operating within these
same forces. Making choices on our own paths
within this understanding brings us freedom.
Freedom to graduate from earth's repetitive cycles, from the predictive matrix.

Freedom is an intangible. It is not an action. It is not an expression of something. It is not a concept that we hold within our mind. It is a vibratory frequency with its own set of harmonics, similar to a musical note. It is a frequency that begins in our heart. We call it up from the deep, vast caverns within where no other can ever reach. It is this frequency that defeats disharmony, mental tussling, restlessness and brings peace.

Freedom is realizing we will never have all the answers, information or knowledge, yet allowing ourselves to be peaceful with this while still playing our part. We have a reason to be here. There is much that we will never know, and yet we have access to all we ever need to know.

Each day is about faith and trust. Not blind faith or intellectual trust. It is faith and trust based on actually experiencing the sensation of our personal connection with Source. This experience tells us we have unlimited choice, and power beyond this world's perception.

*Our Soul-human heart-mind directs our
course and commands our destiny.*

We are awakening out of the mental bondage of
the past thousands of years to a freedom of spirit that encompasses acceptance of all possibility
and potential. When we work through psychic
muck, when we explore a past life, when we puz-
zle out a Soul fragment or life path meaning, we
put a piece of our human self to rest peacefully
within our Soul. We simultaneously free our Soul
to explore anew.

We are like an eternal kaleidoscope. We see the
whole, then we focus on a color, then we focus on
the combinations of colors, until finally we focus
on the whole once again, having found a greater
expansion of our Self in our Soul.

In the tapestry of our lives, there are these golden threads to weave into the cloth:

☙ Our Soul is undying, vast, yet our intimate friend. Our human lives are its chosen forays into experiential states. It lives on after our human body is extinguished to enjoy its next great leap of existence.

☙ We breathe with the breath of the Source that gifts us life. A pulsing that is invisible, yet perceptible. To those who seek it, it is the pure Light-love flowing through our Soul into our heart.

☙ We are our own master. Our Soul will guide us, if we allow it. Our Soul-human heart-mind directs our course and commands our destiny. It is ours to choose whether the way brings suffering or joy, entrapment or freedom.

As these are woven into our stories, we find our freedom. As we seek the connections, the patterns, the dotted pathways, we balance our Self through knowledge, uncover our joy, transcend thought and emotion.

We do not need to find our Self, for we are already here. To know our Self means to know that we are Soul, we are spirit, we are energy fitted into matter. We know how to wield each of these elements for expansion and creation.

'To thine own Self be true' means to take action from the heart, make independent choice, choose unlimited perception, for when expansion is over, so is the magic of life.

Ultimately, where even one of us shakes off the veils of illusion, hundreds and thousands will follow. As we connect to our unlimited power Source, Light fills us and grace completes us as an invisible, quiet stream that flows through us as a golden river.

Joy is in seeking Light. Liberation comes in finding it. Freedom flows through choosing it. Ultimately, its peace sustains all.

All threads of our Soul illuminate. Our human Self is transfigured.

...by Grace we are created...
through Light we are formed...
in Grace we are sustained...

In the beginning...

I walk the sand. As I squish my toes and luxuriate in the soft and the warmth, I smile. I open my eyes, my ears, all my senses and a silent harmonic fills the spaces all around me and within me. I am at peace.

Ah, how I love this place. It is a luscious strip between the vast ocean and the forest and meadows beyond. I look to the waves and see dolphins beckoning me. I could dive into the ocean and play in their vast realms. I could reach to the sky and fly through the stars.

I looked to the forest edge. I could walk its winding pathways and commune with the trees and the animals.

This strip of beach was like a place between the veils of time, space and dimension, where all of possibility dwelled. I could fly through the stars to my Soul's home. I could walk through the forest to my mortal dwelling.

So often I have walked out of the forest to the edge of the water and flown free. When I turn back through the forest it is with sadness and regret, despite the loving creatures who greet me on that path. For beyond that forest, I see the darkness that would subject us to dominance and ignorance.

Yet on this night, the scene was bathed in a different light. A mist of gold. As I reluctantly turned my back on the freedom of the water and the stars, there was a very large, fierce tiger planted solidly in my path, so close I could touch its fur, which shone with unearthly hues.

*It turned its majestic body and beckoned me to fol-
low. We branched to a new path, one that I had
never seen before. I was startled, for after all, this
was my forest! On this path there were no tiny creatures hopping and circling excitedly around me as
was usual. It was quite dark, as if the sun could not
penetrate the thick canopy of trees overhead.*

*We walked forever, or so it seemed. Abruptly we
arrived at the edge of a massive cliff. Tiger nudged
me to the edge, to look beyond the darkness of the
forest. That one tentative step took me from the safe
shadows of my forest to a light that I had never experienced before on this Earth.*

*Spread before me as far as my eye could see was a
valley of such beauty, such richness of colour and
texture, with all imaginable plants, animals – and
people! All calmly going about their tasks. Yet with
such a glow about them. Joyful, serene, peaceful.*

*Tiger nudged me forward again and I found myself
on a path winding its way down to this lovely place.
I hesitated, for my forest was very dear and famil-*

iar to me. Tiger assured me that it would always be there. The beach, the stars, the waves, and the creatures who lived there. They would always be there, and I could visit them at my choosing.

We walked into the valley. As we encountered others, we touched with a smile, a kind word, a helpful hand.

Each gesture of love expanded the golden Light around us all.

In gratitude

To Gilles, always and forever, my loving partner in life, for all you do 'above and beyond' to sustain me in my wanderings.

To Karen Stuth, owner of Satiama Publishing for the depth of your intuitive understanding and unerring accuracy in aiding me to translate concepts to books.

To all the joyous friends it has been my privilege to share the road with over the past few years of producing *The Way* series. You know who you are, scattered far and wide around the world know you are always held close in my heart.

To readers, my thanks for allowing this little book into your hearts.

May we all revel in spiritual freedom and as we journey through the wonder of our life.

Catherine Grace Landry

The journey is not over

Coming soon from Catherine Grace Landry and Satiama Publishing…

The Way of the Grace-filled Heart Cards and Guidebook – a quick and easy, portable format that expands upon the insights of this book.

The Way of the Simple Soul Journal – a companion to the first book of *The Way Series,* providing a guided journaling process to open a clear communication channel with your Soul.

On-line classes and downloadable modules by Catherine Grace Landry that offer sensory, experiential content for you to delve deep into your inner heart to find your personal path to the Light, coming soon from Satiama Publishing (www.satiamapublishing.com.)

Catherine also offers in-person workshops and the intimate *Book Circle* discussions on book's contents.

To stay in touch and see what's coming up, sign up for her newsletter, go to www.catherinegracelandry.com.

For product discounts, sign up for our newsletter.
www.satiamapublishing.com

Catherine loves to hear from her readers!

Contact her at
catherine@catherinegracelandry.com

About the author

Catherine Grace Landry is an award-winning author, teacher, speaker and spiritual guide.

She is a qualified shamanic practitioner, crystal energy therapist and Kundalini yoga instructor.

Follow her on Facebook at her page,
The Way Series with Catherine Landry,
and on her website
www.catherinegracelandry.com.

She can be reached by email at
catherine@catherinegracelandry.com.

The Way of the Grace-filled Heart is her third book in The Way series, preceded by *The Way of the Simple Soul* and *The Way of the Lightkeeper.*